The Olympic FAQ

Jake Ronaldson

Level 3
(1600-word)

IBC パブリッシング

はじめに

　ラダーシリーズは、「はしご (ladder)」を使って一歩一歩上を目指すように、学習者の実力に合わせ、無理なくステップアップできるよう開発された英文リーダーのシリーズです。

　リーディング力をつけるためには、繰り返したくさん読むこと、いわゆる「多読」がもっとも効果的な学習法であると言われています。多読では、「1. 速く 2. 訳さず英語のまま 3. なるべく辞書を使わず」に読むことが大切です。スピードを計るなど、速く読むよう心がけましょう（たとえば TOEIC® テストの音声スピードはおよそ 1 分間に 150 語です）。そして 1 語ずつ訳すのではなく、英語を英語のまま理解するくせをつけるようにします。こうして読み続けるうちに語感がついてきて、だんだんと英語が理解できるようになるのです。まずは、ラダーシリーズの中からあなたのレベルに合った本を選び、少しずつ英文に慣れ親しんでください。たくさんの本を手にとるうちに、英文書がすらすら読めるようになってくるはずです。

《本シリーズの特徴》
- 中学校レベルから中級者レベルまで5段階に分かれています。自分に合ったレベルからスタートしてください。
- クラシックから現代文学、ノンフィクション、ビジネスと幅広いジャンルを扱っています。あなたの興味に合わせてタイトルを選べます。
- 巻末のワードリストで、いつでもどこでも単語の意味を確認できます。レベル1、2では、文中の全ての単語が、レベル3以上は中学校レベル外の単語が掲載されています。
- カバーにヘッドホーンマークのついているタイトルは、オーディオ・サポートがあります。ウェブから購入/ダウンロードし、リスニング教材としても併用できます。

《使用語彙について》

レベル1：中学校で学習する単語約1000語

レベル2：レベル1の単語＋使用頻度の高い単語約300語

レベル3：レベル1の単語＋使用頻度の高い単語約600語

レベル4：レベル1の単語＋使用頻度の高い単語約1000語

レベル5：語彙制限なし

CONTENTS

Introduction 2

Part 1   The Ancient Olympics 5

How did the Olympics begin? 6
Where were the first Olympics held? 9
Why were the ancient Greeks so interested in sports? 10
Why were the Olympics held every four years? 12
What events were held during the Olympics? 14
How were Greek athletes trained? 19
Did the athletes use coaches? 20
Who went to the Olympics? 22
What was it like to watch the Olympics? 23
Who were the judges? 25
How did athletes prepare for the Olympics? 26
How did the athletes prepare before an event? 28
Why didn't the athletes wear any clothes? 29
Why was religion so important in the ancient Olympics? 30
What was the Statue of Zeus like? 31
What kind of prizes did the winners get? 32
What was the "Olympic truce"? 34
Who were the most famous champions of the ancient Olympics? 35
What was the Heraea? 38

Why did the Greeks stop holding the Olympic Games? *38*
What is Olympia like today? *39*

Part 2 The Modern Olympics *43*

How did the modern Olympics start? *44*
What is the International Olympic Committee? *47*
When and where were the first modern Olympics held? *48*
What is "amateurism"? *50*
What happened to amateurism? *51*
What is the Olympic flame? *52*
How many Olympic sports and events are there? *54*
What does *Citius, Altius, Fortius* mean? *55*
What is the meaning of the Olympic rings? *55*
How are sports chosen for the Olympics? *56*
Are the Olympics ever canceled? *57*
How are host cities chosen? *57*
How does technology affect the Olympics? *59*
What countries and cities have hosted the Olympics? *61*
How many athletes compete in the Olympics? *64*
What is "doping"? *64*
What is WADA? *67*
How much do the Olympics cost? *68*
Why were there no women in the first Olympics? *70*
When did women start competing in the Olympics? *71*
How did the Winter Olympics begin? *72*
What is the "Olympic village"? *74*
How many people watch the Olympics around the world? *76*

What happens during the opening and
    closing ceremonies? 76

How much money are Olympic medals worth? 79

What are demonstration sports? 80

What is a "boycott"? 82

Have the Olympics ever been affected by terrorism? 83

Can disabled people compete in the regular Olympics? 85

What are the Paralympics? 86

What are the Youth Olympic Games? 88

Part 3   Medals, Records, and Athletes 91

Who is the greatest Olympic athlete of all time? 92

What country has won the most Olympic medals? 98

Have any athletes ever won medals at both the Winter and
    Summer Olympics? 98

Has any athlete ever set a world record without winning
    a gold medal? 100

Who were some of the toughest athletes ever? 100

Which athletes have competed in the most games? 102

Who was the oldest athlete ever to win a gold medal? 104

Who was the youngest athlete ever to win
    an Olympic event? 105

What are some of the most famous Olympic records? 105

What were some of the most emotional moments in the
    Olympics? 108

Word List 112

【読み始める前に】 オリンピック正式種目

夏のオリンピックで正式種目として認定されているのは2012年現在で26競技302種目です。いくつかの競技は、複数の種別が含まれ、例えば体操競技は、体操競技、新体操、トランポリンがあります。
冬季オリンピックでは7競技（15種別）が採用されています。

- **Archery**　アーチェリー《洋弓ともいい、日本の弓道とは異なる弓術》
- **Athletics**　陸上競技《短距離走、長距離走、リレー、障害走、競歩、走り幅跳び、高飛び、投てきなど》
- **Badminton**　バドミントン《シャトルを打ち合い、得点を競う。1992年から正式種目として採用された》
- **Basketball**　バスケットボール《5対5で競う団体競技。1992年以降アメリカはNBAスターでチームを結成している》
- **Beach Volleyball**　ビーチバレー《砂浜に張ったコートで、2人1組のチームで対戦するバレーボール》
- **Boxing**　ボクシング《専用グローブをつけて戦う拳闘スポーツ。体重別に階級が分けられている》
- **Canoe Slalom**　カヌー・スラローム《急流の川に設置されたゲートを、順番に通過しながらタイムを競う》
- **Canoe Sprint**　カヌー・スプリント《流れのない静水で、直線コースのタイムを競う》
- **Cycling —BMX**　バイシクルモトクロス《障害物が設置されたコースを、車輪の直径20センチ以下の専用自転車で走り、順位を競う》
- **Cycling —Mountain Bike**　マウンテンバイク《未舗装のコースを走り、順位を競う》
- **Cycling —Road**　自転車ロードレース《舗装された道路上のコースを走り順位を競う》
- **Cycling —Track**　自転車トラックレース《競輪コース上を周回し、順位やタイムを競う》

- ☐ **Diving** 飛び込み《水泳競技の一種で、跳ね板飛び込み、高飛び込み、2人で飛び込むシンクロナイズドダイビングなどがある》

- ☐ **Equestrian** —Dressage 馬場馬術《馬術競技の一種で、馬をいかに美しく正確に操れるかを競う》

- ☐ **Equestrian** —Eventing 総合馬術《3日間をかけて馬場馬術、クロスカントリー、障害飛び競技を行う種目》

- ☐ **Equestrian** —Jumping 障害馬術《障害物が設置されたコースを通過し、その技術を競う》

- ☐ **Fencing** フェンシング《西洋の剣術競技、剣の種類ごとにフルーレ、エペ、サーブルの三つの種目がある》

- ☐ **Football** サッカー《オリンピックにおいてはチーム選手は23歳以下と定められ、それ以上の選手は3名までと規定されている》

- ☐ **Gymnastics** —Artistic Gymnastics 体操競技《床運動や器械体操で演技を行い、技や美しさ、安定性などを競う》

- ☐ **Gymnastics** —Rhythmic Gymnastics 新体操《リボンやボールなどの道具を使い、音楽に合わせて演技を行う、芸術性を競う競技》

- ☐ **Gymnastics** —Trampoline Gymnastics トランポリン《トランポリンを使って跳躍し、空中での演技の芸術性と技術を競う競技》

- ☐ **Handball** ハンドボール《7人ずつの2チームがボールを相手チームのゴールに投げ入れて得点を競う種目》

- ☐ **Hockey** ホッケー《先の曲がった棒で相手チームのゴールにボール(パック)を入れて得点を競うチーム競技》

- ☐ **Judo** 柔道《日本の国技の一つでもある武道、体重ごとに階級が分かれている》

- ☐ **Modern Pentathlon** 近代五種競技《1人で射撃・フェンシング・水泳・馬術・ランニングの5競技をこなし、順位を決める複合競技》

- ☐ **Rowing** ボート競技《ボートをこぎ、順位を競う。個人・団体どちらも行われる》

- ☐ **Sailing** セーリング《定められた水上のコースをヨットで回り、順位を競う》

- ☐ **Shooting** 射撃《ライフル、ピストル、散弾銃などの銃器を用いて射撃を行う》
- ☐ **Swimming** 競泳《背泳ぎ、平泳ぎ、バタフライ、自由形、メドレーなど泳法によって種目が分かれ、団体リレーでも競われる》
- ☐ **Synchronized Swimming** シンクロナイズドスイミング《水深のあるプールで音楽に合わせて体を動かし、芸術性や技を競う》
- ☐ **Table Tennis** 卓球《セルロイド製のボールを打ち合って得点を競う球技。個人、ダブルス、団体戦が行われる》
- ☐ **Tae kwon do** テコンドー《多彩な蹴り技が特徴的な格闘技で、韓国の国技》
- ☐ **Tennis** テニス《硬式テニス。ネットをはさんでラケットでボールを打ち合い、得点を競う》
- ☐ **Triathlon** トライアスロン《水泳、自転車競技、長距離走を順番に行う耐久競技》
- ☐ **Volleyball** バレーボール《1チーム6人で、ネット越しに素手でボールを打ち合い、得点を競う》
- ☐ **Water Polo** 水球《プール内のコートで、7名ずつの2チームが、相手ゴールにボールを入れて得点を競う》
- ☐ **Weightlifting** 重量挙げ《両手でバーベルを頭上まで持ち上げ、その重量を競い合う競技。体重ごとの階級分けがある》
- ☐ **Wrestling** レスリング《選手同士が素手で組み合い、相手の両肩を1秒以上床につけることで勝敗を決する》

The Olympic FAQ
Jake Ronaldson

Introduction

Once every four years, thousands of athletes from around the world gather in one city for the Olympic Games. The games are the world's biggest sporting event, and are watched by billions of people. They are a chance to see the best of the best competing in popular events like running, wrestling, swimming, volleyball, skiing, gymnastics, and many more.

But the Olympics are more than just a sporting event. They are a celebration of peace, respect, freedom, fair play, and international friendship.

During the Olympic games, men and women of all races and religions live, eat, and compete together. It does not matter where you were born or what color your skin is. The important things are your speed, strength, technique, and heart. More than anything else, the Olympics are an event that brings the world together. While the Olympics are being held, nearly everyone on Earth is interested in what is happening in that one city. Olympic champions like Nadia Comaneci, Michael Phelps, and Usain Bolt are loved not just in their own countries, but all around the world.

In *The Olympic FAQ*, we will discover the origin of this amazing sporting event in ancient Greece, see how it has changed through history, and learn about the great athletes who have competed in it.

Part 1
The Ancient Olympics

How did the Olympics begin?

There are many legends about how the Olympics began. Here are some of the most famous:

Heracles ....

Some of the oldest legends say that the Olympics were started by the Greek hero Heracles. These stories say that he was the son of the Greek god Zeus. Heracles was said to be the strongest man in the world, and the stories say that he started the games to honor his father because Zeus was the greatest of the Greek gods.

Pelops

Other legends say that the Olympics were started by the great hero Pelops. When he was young, he fell in love with a beautiful woman named Hippodamia. She was the daughter of a king named Oenomaus, and he did not want Hippodamia to get married. Oenomaus said that any man who wanted to marry his daughter had to win a chariot race.

Pelops agreed to the challenge, and he was able to win the race and marry Hippodamia. Oenomaus was killed during the race, and Pelops became the king. The stories say that he started the Olympic Games in honor of his victory.

Iphitos

The most famous legend says that the Olympics were started by a king named Iphitos in 776 BC.

In those days, there were many, many wars

between the cities in Greece, and King Iphitos saw that nearly all of them were fighting one another. There was also a terrible sickness spreading through the country. He did not know what to do, so he visited a place called Delphi.

The ancient Greeks believed that Delphi was a place where the god Apollo spoke to people. Apollo was the son of Zeus, and people went to Delphi to ask questions to him.

Iphitos was told that he should start the Olympics to honor Zeus. If he did that, the wars would stop, and the sickness would go away. Iphitos began holding a running race at Olympia, and that was the beginning of the Olympics.

Unfortunately, no one knows if any of these stories are true. However, we do know that the Greeks measured time based on the Olympic schedule, and they started with the Olympics in 776 BC. This makes it seem likely that Iphitos started the Olympic Games, but they could also be much older.

Part 1 The Ancient Olympics

Where were the first Olympics held?

The first Olympic Games were held in Olympia, Greece. Olympia was the home of a very famous temple where people worshipped the god Zeus.

Zeus was the greatest of the Greek gods, and the Olympic Games were held to honor him.

Every four years, people from all over Greece traveled to Olympia to see running races, boxing and wrestling, discus and javelin throwing, and many other events as well. Olympia was a very famous place, but people had to travel a very long way because it was far from other towns

Olympia, in Ancient Greece

and cities in Greece. It was hundreds of kilometers from the capital city of Athens, and the nearest city, Elis, was more than 60 kilometers away.

Olympia was in a beautiful country area, and the temple buildings were made of marble. There were temples for Zeus, his wife Hera, and his mother Rhea. It also had many statues and monuments to the other gods, and there were some for the great Olympic athletes as well.

Olympia also had a running track, a wrestling school, a gymnasium, and a horse-racing track. It may sound strange to have temples and a wrestling school beside each other, but the Olympics were a festival where people honored Zeus by trying to be the best in sports.

Why were the ancient Greeks so interested in sports?

The ancient Greeks loved sports. The famous Greek poet Homer wrote, "There is no greater glory for any man alive, than that which he wins by his hands and feet." Sports were one of the most important parts of a person's education, and every city and town had a place called a gymnasium for athletic training.

One reason that the ancient Greeks were so interested in sports was that for many people, everything in life was a competition.

The word *agon* was very popular in ancient Greece. It meant "competition" or "contest," and it was common in all parts of Greek society.

The Greeks always wanted to see who was the best at everything. They had drama contests, pottery contests, speech-making contests, poetry contests, and sculpture contests. There were also eating contests, beauty contests (for both men and women!), and even kissing contests. The ancient Greeks even had races and other sports contests at weddings and funerals.

Another reason that the Greeks played so many sports was that there were a lot of wars in Greece. Greece is one country today, but long ago, it was a collection of cities. The cities were always at war with one another, and sports were good training for war.

For example, the javelin was an important weapon in war, so it was good practice to throw it in sport. Armies had to march long distances, so running helped to make them strong and healthy. Boxing and wrestling were important skills to help men survive in battles.

One final reason for the Greek love of sports was that they loved beautiful bodies. They believed that a beautiful body was a gift from the gods and that people should train their bodies through sports to make themselves healthy and beautiful.

Why were the Olympics held every four years?

The Olympics were not the only important sporting contest that was held in ancient Greece. They were the first and the most important games, but they were also just one part of what was called the Panhellenic Games.

The word *pan* means "all" and *hellene* means "Greece." The Panhellenic Games got their name because they were contests that brought people together from all over Greece.

The Olympics were held every four years so that athletes could go to all four of the Panhellenic Games. In those days, it was very difficult to travel, and it would have been very hard to go to all of the games in one year. The other three events were the Pythian Games at Delphi, the Isthmian Games in Corinth, and the Nemean Games in Nemea.

The Pythian Games were held for the sun god Apollo, and like the Olympics, they were held every four years. The Nemean Games were every two years and were held for the god Zeus. Like the Nemean Games, the Isthmian Games were held every two years, but they were held for the sea god Poseidon.

The games took place in a four-year cycle called an Olympiad. The Olympic Games were held in year one, and then the next year, the Nemean and Isthmian Games were held in different months. The Pythian Games were held in year three, and then the Nemean and Isthmian Games were held again in year four.

What events were held during the Olympics?

Some of the events were the same as in the modern Olympics. There were races, wrestling, boxing, javelin throwing, and the discus. But there were no team sports. There were no ball sports, no swimming races, and no winter events.

The ancient Greeks only wanted to see events that were somehow related to fighting or war, and they always wanted to see people competing alone to see who was the best.

At first, the Olympics had only one event. It was a running race of about 190 meters, and it was called the *stade*. Over time, more events were added, and in the end there were 18 events at the ancient Olympics:

Chariot races....................

The chariot races were the first events at every Olympics, and they were held on the second day. They were one of the most popular events but also the most dangerous.

The chariot races were held on a special track called a *hippodrome*. In one of the races, there were 40 chariots pulled by four horses each, and they ran on a narrow track just 90 meters wide. At each end of the track, there was a 180 degree turn, and this was always the most dangerous part of the race.

The horses ran at very high speed, and if the driver wanted to win the race, he could not slow down very much for the turns. The turns were so dangerous that teams of men waited at the sides of the track to run out and pull the driver to safety when there was a crash.

During one amazing and dangerous race, there were so many accidents that just one chariot was able to finish!

Chariot races
(photo: Marie-Lan Nguyen)

The pentathlon ....

After the chariot races, people moved to the stadium to see the pentathlon. It was a contest with five different events: the discus, the javelin, the long jump, wrestling, and running. The most unusual part of the pentathlon was the long jump. It was not like the modern long jump at all.

The pentathlon
(photo: MatthiasKabel)

The jumpers carried weights that helped them to jump farther, and flute music was played during the event. The athletes did not run before their jump. Instead, they moved their arms and bodies with the rhythm of the music until they felt ready. It looked very strange, but it is said that they were able to jump long distances using this technique.

The boys' events ....

On the afternoon of day three, teenage boys competed in many of the same events that the men did on the other days. They had races and also did wrestling, boxing, and the *pankration*.

Running races

Day four was the day of races. The Olympics started as a running race, so the fans got very excited about these events. There were long- and short-distance races, but surprisingly there was no marathon.

The marathon is a modern race, and it comes from a Greek story about a man who ran 42 kilometers to tell Athens that Greece had won a great battle against its enemies, but it was never in the ancient Olympics.

Fighting events

The races finished in the morning, and in the afternoon, it was time for wrestling, boxing, and the *pankration*.

The sports of boxing and wrestling were very popular events at the ancient

The pankration
(photo: Marie-Lan Nguyen)

Olympics, just as they are at the modern games today. However, modern sports fans might be shocked to see the boxing matches. Boxers often lost teeth, and a few times, they were even killed.

An event called the *pankration* was even scarier. It was a fight between two men, and they were allowed to break each other's bones, hit or kick each other in the head, and use many other dirty fighting techniques. There was only one rule. They were not allowed to put their fingers in the other person's eyes. Men were often killed in this event, but it was the most popular of the fighting sports.

The race in armor

On the fifth and final day, a very strange race was held. It was called the *hoplitodromia*. It was a race in which the athletes wore heavy suits of armor. They had to run around

The race in armor
(photo: MatthiasKabel)

the stadium two times, and they often fell or bumped into one another. Many Greeks thought it was very funny.

How were Greek athletes trained?

Greek athletes trained for the Olympics in a place called a gymnasium. The word "gymnasium" is still used today, and in English it means a large room in a school or other building that is used for playing sports. But our modern gymnasiums are very different from the ones that the Greeks used.

The Greek gymnasium was a public sports ground, and it was made up of both buildings and outdoor areas. There was usually a running track, and it was often by a river so that men could practice swimming.

But the gymnasium was for more than just sports. The gymnasium was a school, a library, and a meeting place where Greek men came to spend time together. In fact, it was one of the most important parts of any Greek town or city. Many gymnasiums had beautiful gardens as well. The gymnasium in Athens even had a museum of natural science.

Gymnasiums were places where young boys came to learn how to read, write, and do mathematics, and they were also places where men trained for war.

Many Greek boys started going to gymnasiums when they were six years old. The coaches there watched the young boys very carefully, and if they seemed to be good athletes, they got special training.

And if they were really good, when they were older, they were given a chance to compete in the Olympic Games.

Did the athletes use coaches?

The athletes in the Olympics were professionals, and they had professional coaches, just as today's athletes do. These coaches were called *paidotribai*.

Most of the coaches were retired athletes,

and they were usually over 40 years old. They taught the athletes how to do well in their sports, but the coaches also had other types of information as well. Many of them were experts in anatomy, healthy eating, medicine, and physiotherapy.

Coaches had a very important relationship with the athletes, and they often helped the athletes to win in difficult situations.

In 520 BC, the famous boxer Glaucus was about to give up in his fight, but his coach shouted, "Give him one for the plow."

The coach's words made Glaucus remember that he first showed how strong he was when he lived on a farm. He was able to straighten a metal plow part with only his hands. People who saw him do it told him that someday he would be a great sporting champion.

When Glaucus heard the coach's words, he found new strength inside himself and hit the other boxer so hard that he ended the fight with just one punch.

Who went to the Olympics?

Everyone in Greece wanted to see the Olympics. Each time the games were held, people traveled from all over the country to see them.

The Olympic stadium held about 40,000 people, but far more than that came to Olympia. It is said that about 70,000 people went to Olympia for the five days of the Olympic Games.

All kinds of people, rich and poor, young and old, came to see the Olympics, but most of them were men. This was because married women were not allowed in.

Most of the people who watched the Olympics were Greeks, but some people came from faraway places like Spain.

People did not just go to Olympia to watch sports. There were also beauty contests, reading contests, and eating races. People could get massages, watch dances, and listen to people making speeches. The plays of famous writers were performed on the steps of the temples. There were also people selling all kinds of things, from paintings to shark's teeth.

The great writers Herodotus and Thucydides read their books for the first time at Olympia. Many people heard them read, and when these people went back to their home cities, they told everyone about the great books that had been read. Herodotus and Thucydides became two of the most famous men in Greece because they went to the Olympics.

Artists also loved Olympia, and they did many famous paintings and sculptures of the athletes. The statues and sculptures were beautiful, and today they are some of the greatest art treasures in the world.

What was it like to watch the Olympics?

The Olympics were an amazing event, but it was not always easy to visit them. One of the biggest problems for spectators was finding a place to stay.

There was only one hotel at Olympia, and it was only for very important people. The others had to camp in the area around the temples. Rich people had large tents filled with expensive goods and had many types of delicious food to eat. But ordinary people had to stay in small wooden shelters or sleep outdoors under trees.

During the Olympics, the air was bad because of all the smoke from cooking fires, and there was not enough water for everyone. Most people were dirty because there was not enough water to wash with, and they smelled very bad.

Because of the great numbers of people, it was easy for sicknesses to spread. Sometimes many people died from sicknesses at Olympia.

It was also difficult to see the events. There were no tickets or seat reservations, and sometimes thousands of people tried to crowd into very small spaces. Officials had to use whips to control the crowds.

Another problem was that the Olympics were held in summer, so it was very hot. Every day many people got heatstroke, and some of them died.

People who watched the Olympics suffered

a lot, but it was also very exciting. The Greeks loved sports, and at Olympia they could see the greatest athletes competing against one another. People said everyone should see the Olympics once in their lives.

Who were the judges?

At the first Olympic Games, there was only one judge. King Iphitos started the race and made sure that no one cheated. But later, as the games grew and new events were added, more judges became needed. After a while, the number of judges grew to 10.

All the judges came from one city. The city was called Elis, and it was the nearest city to Olympia. The judges were rich landowners, and at first the job was passed down from father to son. Later, however, the judges were elected.

The Olympic judges were called Hellanodikai. There were three judges for the horse riding events, three for the pentathlon, and three for all the other events. The tenth judge was the most important, and his job was to supervise all the others. The judges did more than just make sure that everyone followed the rules during the games. They also worked to organize the games, and they took part in the many ceremonies as well.

For one month before the Olympics started, the judges had one other very important job to do. They had to work hard as trainers for the athletes. Their job was to watch over the final month of training for all of the athletes who were going to compete in the Olympics.

How did athletes prepare for the Olympics?

One month before the Olympics started, all the athletes had to go to Elis, the nearest city to Olympia. There, they took part in a strict training program. The training was very tough. Greece is very hot in the summer, and the athletes exercised for many hours every day.

It was believed that the athletes were training to compete in front of the god Zeus, so it was expected that the athletes would give a 100 percent effort every minute of the day. If the athletes did not do what they were told, or if they did not make enough effort, the Hellanodikai whipped them.

The judges watched all of the athletes very carefully, and if they decided that one of them was not good enough, they did not let him compete in the games.

When the training was finished, the athletes all gathered together for a ceremony. Two days before the games began, the Hellanodikai made a speech to them. They told the athletes that if they had exercised hard, had not been lazy, and had not done anything wrong, then they should go to Olympia with courage. But if they had not done so, then they should leave Elis and stay away from the Olympics.

After that, the athletes and judges began the 60 kilometer walk to Olympia. The judges wore fancy purple robes, and the athletes wore white. They were joined by the athletes' trainers and family members, and many people came to see them as they traveled to the games.

How did the athletes prepare before an event?

Before their event, the men put olive oil on their bodies. One reason was that Greece is a very hot country, and the men did not want to sweat out the water in their bodies. The olive oil helped to stop the men from sweating when they were exercising.

However, some people think that there may have been a more important reason. We know that olives were an important symbol of Zeus, and there were many sacred olive trees at Olympia. It seems likely that the athletes hoped this sacred oil would protect them from injuries and defeat. After putting on olive oil, the men also put powder on their bodies. It was probably used so that they would not be slippery from the oil.

Before the event started, the athletes would do various warm-up exercises. Surprisingly, many of the exercises were done with flute music. Men would jump up and down on the spot, do high kicks, and lift weights, all in time with the music.

Why didn't the athletes wear any clothes?

At first, the athletes in the Olympics wore loincloths. However, at some time they stopped wearing them, and no one knows why.

One story says that during a race, a runner's loincloth fell off, and he fell because of it. After that, people were afraid that the same thing would happen to them, so they started to run without wearing any clothes.

Another story says that there was a runner named Orsippos of Megara, and he believed that he could run faster without his loincloth. He stopped wearing it, and he won first place in the sprint in 720 BC. After that, other people started to copy him.

One important reason that athletes did not wear any clothes may be that the Olympics were a religious event. The games were a performance to make the gods happy. The athletes may have wanted to show their beautiful bodies.

Surprisingly, it was not only the athletes who did not wear clothes. The Olympic rules said that the coaches could not wear clothes either.

The reason is that in the year 404 BC, a married women had come into the Olympic stadium wearing a trainer's clothes. Married women were not allowed to watch the Olympics, and it caused a big scandal. After that, a rule was made that the coaches could not wear clothes, to stop women from sneaking in.

Why was religion so important in the ancient Olympics?

Religion was very important in the lives of all Greek people. They believed that gods made the sun come up in the morning, made rain fall, and caused the wind to blow.

The ancient Greeks also thought that if someone got sick, it was because the gods were angry at the person.

People prayed to gods all the time, and they also killed animals at temples to try to make the gods happy. Zeus was the king of these important gods, and the Olympics were a festival to honor him. The Greeks believed that he loved to watch athletes competing.

It is important to remember that religion was more important than sports at the ancient Olympics. If you asked a visitor what the highlight of the games was, he would probably tell you that it was the sacrifice of oxen.

On the third day, 100 white oxen were killed. The Greeks believed that killing these animals would make Zeus happy. If Zeus was happy, he would keep Greece safe from its enemies, bring rain to the farms, and protect the weak.

What was the Statue of Zeus like?

Religion was so important at Olympia that the Greeks built an amazing statue of Zeus there. Like the Great Pyramid of Giza in Egypt, it was one of the Seven Wonders of the Ancient World.

The statue of Zeus was 12 meters high and sat on a giant wooden throne that was covered with jewels. Zeus's body was made of ivory, and his clothes were made of gold. The statue was beautiful and frightening at the same time.

Statue of Zeus

Ancient writers say it was so amazing that people almost always became silent when they saw it.

Visiting the statue of Zeus and praying at his temple were just as important for the visitors as watching the games.

What kind of prizes did the winners get?

Today's Olympic winners get medals made out of gold, silver, or bronze. But in the ancient Olympics, the winners got only wreaths made out of olive branches. The olive wreath was called a *kotinos*. The *kotinos* was not worth any money, but it was a very important prize. There were a lot of olive trees at Olympia, and they were a symbol of Zeus.

Although the olive wreath was a very simple prize, the winners knew that after the games they would have chances to get a lot of money. Many of the cities paid men who lived there to go to the Olympics. The cities knew that if their athletes won, everyone would think that they were a strong, powerful city. For this reason, they often paid their athletes a lot of money for winning.

If a man won the Olympic Games, he was given a parade in his home city, and he would be a hero there for the rest of his life. He would have so much money that he probably would not have to work again, and he would become a hero to the local people. Getting an olive wreath was a great honor, but the men who were second and third got nothing. Today, many athletes are very happy to get a silver or bronze medal, but the Greeks felt very differently. They wanted to win, and they thought that being second or third was just as bad as being last.

If an athlete did not win his event, he thought that he had been embarrassed in front of the whole of Greece. Sometimes, men who were second killed themselves because they thought losing was shameful.

Olive wreaths are still given to event winners at the Olympics today.

What was the "Olympic truce"?

Ancient Greece was not just one country. There were hundreds of cities in Greece, and they were like small countries.

The Greeks spoke the same language, and they believed in the same gods, but they were always fighting. These small cities fought so many wars that it is impossible to count them all.

But there was one time when all the fighting stopped. For one month before and after the Olympics, there were no wars anywhere in Greece. Messengers were sent out to travel all over Greece. They announced when the Olympics were going to be held, and also told people that there could be no fighting before, during, and after the games.

The Olympics were a very important religious event, and people traveled from all over Greece to see them. The Olympics were a time to honor the god Zeus, and during this time all the wars stopped. The main reason was so that all the athletes and spectators could travel safely to Olympia.

This was also the beginning of the modern idea that the Olympics should help to bring peace to the world.

Who were the most famous champions of the ancient Olympics?

There were many famous champions in the Olympics, and their names were known all over Greece. Here are a few of them:

Coroibos ....

The first Olympic champion was a man named Coroibos. When the Olympics started, there was only one event, and it was called the *stade*. It was a race in which athletes ran around a 190 meter track.

In 776, Coroibos became the first man to win it, but he was not a famous soldier or a rich man. He was a cook. Except for that, no one knows much about him.

Milo of Croton ....

Many people today still know the story of Milo of Croton, who was famous for his unusual training method. He was born on a farm, and he did not have a chance to go to a gymnasium. He wanted to make himself stronger, so he decided to pick up a young bull calf every day. The bull calf grew heavier little by little, and finally he was able to pick up a huge bull. He won the wrestling event in five different Olympic Games over a period of 20 years! This record has still not been broken today.

Polites ....

Many people believe that the greatest Olympic runner ever was a man named Polites. He did something that has never been done since. He won both the shortest Olympic race and the longest one. First, he won the *stade*, the same 190 meter race won by Coroibos. Then, later that same day, he won the *dolichos*, a long-distance race that was probably about 3.8 kilometers.

Runners who are good at running very fast usually have a different kind of muscle than runners who are good at running for a long time, and the way they train is very different.

It is incredible that a man could be born with a body that was able to win two events that are so different. No one has ever done something like this in the modern Olympics. It happened only once in the thousand-year history of the ancient Olympics, and we will be lucky if it happens again in the next thousand years of the modern Olympics.

What was the Heraea?

The Heraea were like the Olympics, but they were only for young women. The Olympics were to honor the god Zeus, but the Heraea were to honor his wife Hera. They were held every four years, probably sometime before the Olympics. They took place at Olympia too, but there was only one event.

It was a race, and the distance was five-sixths of the length of the Olympic stadium. In the men's races, they ran all the way around the stadium, but the women's race was shorter because people believed that women take shorter steps than men do.

Winning the Heraea was a great honor, and the girls who won it could put their pictures in the temple of Hera at Olympia.

Why did the Greeks stop holding the Olympic Games?

Greece became a province of the Roman Empire in 146 BC. However, for many years, the

Part 1 The Ancient Olympics

Romans allowed the Olympics to continue.

Originally, only Greeks could compete in the Olympics, but after Greece became part of the Roman Empire, Romans were allowed to compete too.

It became very popular for Romans to travel to Greece to see the Olympics, and many of them competed in the games as well. Later, people from all over the Empire began coming to the Olympics.

However, in the year 394 AD, the Christian emperor Theodosius decided to cancel the Olympics. He and many other Romans thought that everyone should believe in the Christian god, and he did not want people to go to an event where another god was worshipped, so he canceled them.

When the last Olympics were held in 394 AD, the games were 1,170 years old.

What is Olympia like today?

Surprisingly, for hundreds of years after the

Olympic Games ended, no one knew where Olympia was. The temple of Zeus was destroyed by Christians, and Olympia was later buried by floods and earthquakes.

No one could find Olympia until a British man named Richard Chandler discovered it in 1766. Some Greek farmers found pieces of marble in a field, and Chandler realized that it was Olympia.

Later, in the year 1875, German archaeologists traveled to Greece and began working to find all of the old buildings at Olympia. The Germans discovered the temple of Zeus and also found many old statues.

Today, Olympia has become one of the most

German excavation of Olympia, Greece.

popular tourist attractions in Greece. You can see the ruins of many of the old buildings, and there is an excellent museum with thousands of pieces of beautiful art.

Of course, the most popular attraction is the old stadium. You can even see the old starting line for the races, and many people run around the track, imaging what it must have been like for the Olympic athletes thousands of years ago.

Part 2
The Modern Olympics

How did the modern Olympics start?

The modern Olympic Games that we know today were started by a man named Pierre de Coubertin. He was born in Paris, France, on January 1, 1863.

Coubertin was very interested in education, but he wanted to do more than just teach people to read and write. He believed that sports could be very important in improving people's characters.

Coubertin believed that sports taught people how to cooperate, respect other people, and work hard. He thought that if everyone was made stronger by competing against others in sports, it could make the world a better place.

In 1890, Coubertin had an experience that changed his life. He went to England and saw an event called the Much Wenlock Olympic Games. Much Wenlock was a small village, and their "Olympics" was mostly just games like cricket, a bicycle race, and even events for children. It was not international, and the competition was not at a high level.

But seeing the Much Wenlock Olympics gave Coubertin a great idea. He decided that he should start the Olympics again. He liked the Much Wenlock Olympics a lot, but he wanted the games to be international, and he thought that the competition should be much more serious.

Pierre de Coubertin

In those days, people were very interested in the ancient Olympics because Olympia had been rediscovered and archaeologists were busy excavating the ruins. In 1894, Coubertin formed a new organization called the International Olympic Committee (IOC). The IOC had members from various countries, and they began making plans to hold the first modern Olympics in 1896. They planned to bring them back to Greece and hold the Olympic Games in Athens.

Coubertin worked hard to organize the Athens Olympics, and he wrote the Olympic Charter. It is a document that explains the rules and guidelines for the Olympics and the IOC.

Coubertin also made many important decisions about what the games should be like and how the athletes should behave. Throughout his life, Coubertin promoted the Olympics wherever he went.

Coubertin became the second president of the IOC. He continued to work with the IOC until he died in Geneva, Switzerland, on September 2, 1937.

What is the International Olympic Committee?

The International Olympic Committee (IOC) is the group that organizes the Olympics. They do things such as choosing the host cities, making policies for the Olympics, and promoting the Olympics around the world. The headquarters of the IOC is in Lausanne, Switzerland, and the IOC has 205 members.

Many people think that the IOC just works on the Olympics, but it actually does much more than that. The true purpose of the IOC is to build a better world through sport. For example, the IOC asks host cities to make sure that the facilities they build for the Olympics do not harm the environment, and it makes sure that the Olympics send a message about the importance of protecting the environment to the people who watch them.

Another thing that the IOC does is to encourage more women to play sports. The IOC works with each country and each sport's Olympic committee to be sure that the sport is open to women. It also tries to encourage more women to take part in sports at a high level.

Perhaps the most important thing that the IOC does, however, is to encourage world peace. By bringing together athletes from nearly every country in the world, they are helping to promote understanding among people of different countries.

The Olympics show men and women of all different religions, countries, and races competing against one another in an atmosphere of fairness and respect. When people around the world see this, they learn about the Olympic dream of a world where people are not racist, accept other people's religions, and do not fight in wars.

When and where were the first modern Olympics held?

The first games of the modern Olympics were held in Athens, Greece, in 1896. Athens was chosen because Greece was the home of the original Olympics, and everyone thought that

The 1896 Summer Olympics in Athens, Greece

The opening ceremonies of the 1896 Summer Olympics.

the modern Olympics should begin there.

The Olympic Games started on April 5 and continued for 10 days. The events included running races, lawn tennis, swimming, diving, fencing, cycling, rowing, and a yacht race.

Athletes came from 14 different countries. Most of them were from Europe, America, or Australia. It was the first time in the history of the world that so many countries had come together for a sporting event.

Many of the events were held at Panathinaiko Stadium, and it was the largest crowd of people ever to watch a sporting event.

Many Greek people were interested in the Olympics, and on the last day, the king of Greece came to give prizes to the winners. They were given wreaths made from olive trees growing in Olympia. There were 44 winners: 11 Americans, 10 Greeks, 7 Germans, 5 French, 3 English, 2 Australians, 1 Dane, and 1 Swiss.

What is "amateurism"?

When Pierre de Coubertin started the modern Olympics, he believed that athletes should never be paid. For him, the purpose of playing sports was to make oneself a better person.

Pierre de Coubertin loved the ancient Greek idea that there were no money prizes at the Olympics. He and many others wanted the games to be a pure competition. They thought that if some people received money to play sports, it would not be fair because those people would be able to spend more time training and have better equipment than the other athletes.

What happened to amateurism?

For many years, only amateurs were allowed to compete in the Olympics, but it caused many problems. For example, the great athlete Jim Thorpe won two gold medals at the 1912 Summer Olympics in Stockholm, Sweden, but it was later discovered that he had played professional baseball in the past.

Thorpe lost his medals, but many people were very angry because he was a great champion, and he was not a member of a professional team when he won his medals.

Throughout the 20th century, athletes got better and better, and it was necessary to spend more time training to be successful.

Professional athletes were getting rich, and many Olympic athletes wondered why they were working so hard without getting any money for it. Also, after World War II, communist countries like Russia and China spent a lot of money to support their team members, but these athletes were still called "amateurs" at the Olympics.

Olympic Athletes also began to find tricky ways to get money. Sometimes companies paid them a lot of money to wear clothes with their names on them during the games, but the money was not paid to them directly, or it was paid later, after the person quit the sport.

The IOC decided that it was time to give up the idea of amateurism in 1972. They decided to let each sport make its own rules about amateurism, and today, there are very few sports that do not let professionals compete at the Olympics.

What is the Olympic flame?

The Olympic flame is one of the most famous symbols of the Olympic Games. It started at the ancient Olympics, and it comes from the famous myth of Prometheus. In this story, Prometheus stole fire from the god Zeus and gave it to humans. Many Greek temples had fires which were always kept burning, and during the ancient Olympics, a fire was lit using the sun's rays. The fire was kept burning during the whole of the games.

The custom of the Olympic flame was born again at the 1928 Summer Olympics in Amsterdam, in the Netherlands, and the torch relay started with the 1936 Summer Olympics in Berlin, Germany.

Several months before the start of each Olympic Games, a special ceremony is held in a temple in Olympia, Greece. Priestesses light a torch using the light of the sun and a special mirror. The fire is lit in this way because the sun's light represents purity. From Olympia, the torch is carried to the host city. It is carried across the ocean on airplanes or ships, and when it arrives in the host country, it is usually carried by runners. Hundreds of people are chosen to

The Olympic flame is lit for the first time during the Amsterdam Olympics in 1928 (left), and the first torch relay in the 1936 Berlin Olympics (right).

carry the Olympic flame.

Sometimes, the Olympic flame is carried in unusual ways. It has been carried by rowers in Australia, by dragon boat in Hong Kong, and by dogsled in Canada.

In the year 2004, the Summer Olympics were held in Athens, Greece, but the flame went all around world. It was carried more than 78,000 kilometers by about 11,300 runners!

At the end of the torch relay, the Olympic flame enters the Olympic stadium during the opening ceremony of the games. When the fire is lit in the stadium, the Olympics have officially begun.

How many Olympic sports and events are there?

The number of Summer Olympic sports has grown from just 9 in the 1896 Olympics to 26 in the 2012 London Olympics. The IOC has a rule that there cannot be more than 28 sports, and in 2016, 2 more will be added, so after that there will be no room for new sports unless others are removed.

Many of the sports have more than one event. At the Beijing Olympics in 2008, there were 302 different events.

In the past, many different kinds of sports have been part of the Olympics. Cricket, croquet, and even the tug of war have all been Olympic sports at some time.

What does *Citius, Altius, Fortius* mean?

The motto of the Olympics is *Citius, Altius, Fortius*. The words are Latin and mean "faster, higher, stronger." Pierre de Coubertin had a friend named Henri Didon, and Didon thought of this motto for a sports competition that he organized in 1891. Pierre de Coubertin liked it very much, and it became the Olympic motto in 1924.

What is the meaning of the Olympic rings?

The Olympic rings are one of the most famous symbols in the world. They were designed by

Pierre de Coubertin in 1912, and the rings represent the five parts of the world that take part in the Olympics. There is one ring for each of the five main continents: Europe, Asia, Africa, Oceania, and the Americas. (North and South America are represented with one ring.) The rings are all joined together, and this represents all of the different parts of the world coming together for the Olympics.

How are sports chosen for the Olympics?

It is very difficult for a sport to be accepted into the Olympics. The most important thing is that a sport has to be popular all over the world.

For a men's summer sport, it must be played in at least 75 countries, and for a women's summer sport it must be played in at least 40 countries.

The sport must also have official rules, an international organization that controls it, and a world championship.

Are the Olympics ever canceled?

The only times that the Olympics were canceled were during World War I and World War II. Berlin, Germany, was scheduled to host the games in 1916. Tokyo, Japan, was scheduled to host them in 1940. London, England, was scheduled to host them in 1944.

How are host cities chosen?

During the first modern Olympic Games in 1896, it was very easy to choose the host city. The games started in Greece, so the IOC chose Athens. Since then, however, the decision has become much more difficult.

These days, many cities want to host the Olympics, and there is a lot of tough competition.

Cities that want to host the Olympics have to spend a lot of money in their campaign to get the Olympics. Many spend $100 million or more.

The IOC studies 18 different things when it decides which city to give the Olympics to. It thinks about the city's stadiums and facilities for the athletes, its transportation system, its security plan, how much the people of the city support the Olympics, and many other things.

Cities that want to become a host city have to spend years preparing. They make many presentations, and they also invite members of the IOC to visit them. Of course, after all the preparations, if a city is not selected, it loses all the money that it spent, and it can be very embarrassing.

However, there are some very good reasons for trying to become an Olympic city. One is that the Olympics can be very good for the economy. Before an Olympics, many cities improve their public transportation systems and make their public facilities nicer. This spending can often stimulate the economy. Cities can also get a lot of money from tourism and from Olympic sponsors.

One other reason that some cities want to host the Olympics is that it is a good way to show the world that they are a part of a modern country.

2008 Summer Olympics in Beijing

When Tokyo hosted the Olympics in 1964, people were able to see that Japan was a modern, peaceful country. The 2008 Olympics in Beijing were also important for showing that China had changed since the days of Communism.

How does technology affect the Olympics?

People have been getting bigger, stronger, and healthier over the past 100 years, and for this reason, many new Olympic records are being set every time the Olympic Games are held. However, there is also another reason for the number of new world records that are being set: technology.

Modern sports equipment, clothes, swimming pools, running tracks, and many other things are giving today's athletes a big advantage. For example, the poles used for the pole vault have changed a lot over the past 100 years. At first, they were made of wood, but in the 1950s, they began to be made with aluminum and fiberglass.

Fiberglass poles made it a lot easier for athletes to jump very high, and since they were introduced, more and more world records have been set. In fact, world records have gone up by over two meters in the past 100 years!

Running records have also been helped by technology. The shoes that athletes wear are very light, and they give excellent support to their feet.

Many athletes also wear special body suits that help them to move more easily through the wind. The tracks, too, are specially designed to make it easier to run without wasting energy, and they also help to prevent injuries.

Some people say that it is not fair for athletes to use so much technology. Athletes from rich countries in Europe and North America often have much better equipment than athletes from poorer countries in Africa and Asia.

Although it is true that technology gives some athletes an advantage, it can also make sports fairer. For example, in the sport of tae kwon do, all athletes now wear sensors on their bodies.

It can be difficult to see if a punch or kick really hit a person, but the sensors can tell whether a point has been scored or not. This helps to prevent mistakes by the judges.

It seems that technology is going to continue to have a big effect on sports in the Olympics in the future.

What countries and cities have hosted the Olympics?

The Summer Olympics have been held 26 times since the Olympics began in 1896, and the Winter Olympics have been held 21 times since 1924.

Summer Olympic Games Sites
1896–Athens, Greece
1900–Paris, France

1904–St. Louis, United States
1908–London, United Kingdom
1912–Stockholm, Sweden
1920–Antwerp, Belgium
1924–Paris, France
1928–Amsterdam, Netherlands
1932–Los Angeles, United States
1936–Berlin, Germany
1948–London, United Kingdom
1952–Helsinki, Finland
1956–Melbourne, Australia
1960–Rome, Italy
1964–Tokyo, Japan
1968–Mexico City, Mexico
1972–Munich, West Germany (now Germany)
1976–Montreal, Canada
1980–Moscow, USSR (now Russia)
1984–Los Angeles, United States
1988–Seoul, South Korea
1992–Barcelona, Spain
1996–Atlanta, United States
2000–Sydney, Australia
2004–Athens, Greece

2008–Beijing, China
2012–London, United Kingdom
2016–Rio de Janeiro, Brazil

Winter Olympic Games Sites
1924–Chamonix, France
1928–St. Moritz, Switzerland
1932–Lake Placid, United States
1936–Berlin, Germany
1948–St. Moritz, Switzerland
1952–Oslo, Norway
1956–Cortina d'Ampezzo, Italy
1960–Squaw Valley, United States
1964–Innsbruck, Austria
1968–Grenoble, France
1972–Sapporo, Japan
1976–Innsbruck, Austria
1980–Lake Placid, United States
1984–Sarajevo, Yugoslavia
    (now Bosnia and Herzegovina)
1988–Calgary, Canada
1992–Albertville, France
1994–Lillehammer, Norway

1998–Nagano, Japan

2002–Salt Lake City, United States

2006–Torino, Italy

2010–Vancouver, Canada

2014–Sochi, Russia

2018–Pyeongchang, South Korea

How many athletes compete in the Olympics?

Every Olympics is different. At the first Olympics in Athens, Greece, in 1896, there were just 245 athletes, and more than 200 of them came from Greece.

Today, almost every country in the world competes in the Olympics. There were 203 countries competing at the 2008 Olympics in Beijing, and there were 11,028 athletes from those 203 countries.

What is "doping"?

Many athletes have discovered that they can train harder and perform better by taking performance-enhancing drugs (PEDs). These are drugs that make an athlete's muscles bigger, stop them from feeling pain, give them more endurance, or have other effects that help them to win in sports. Using these drugs is called "doping."

Many people think that athletes started using PEDs in the Olympics very recently, but it has actually been happening almost since the Olympics began.

During the 1904 Summer Olympics in St. Louis, in the United States, the winner of the marathon, Thomas Hicks, was given a drug called strychnine to give him more energy when he began to get very tired during the race. The drug had a strong effect on him, and it probably helped him to win the race. However, in those days people thought that it was important to take drugs during the marathon because it was such a difficult event.

The real problems with PEDs began in the 1950s. Athletes discovered that PEDs called steroids could help them to make their muscles larger. Weightlifters from Russia began to use them first, but they were soon copied by athletes from the United States. After that, athletes from around the world began to use PEDs.

In the 1960 Olympics, a Danish cyclist named Knud Enemark Jensen fell off his bicycle and later died. It was discovered that he had taken amphetamines before the race.

After Jensen died, people began to understand that PEDs were a very serious problem in the Olympics. Many sports began to ban the use of PEDs, and in 1967 the IOC made strict rules saying that PEDs could not be used in the Olympic Games.

The rules said that if athletes were caught using PEDs, they would lose their medals. Soon after the new rules were made, an athlete named Hans-Gunnar Liljenwall lost his bronze medal in the pentathlon because it was discovered that he had alcohol in his body.

The use of PEDs such as steroids spread even more during the 1970s, and there was a lot of pressure on athletes to use them.

Many athletes train for their whole lives, and

they want to win a medal more than anything else in the world. In those days, in some sports most of the athletes from the Soviet Union used drugs. It was discovered that PEDs were even being given to 11-year-old East German girls.

The most famous drug scandal in Olympic history happened at the 1988 Summer Olympics in Seoul, South Korea. A Canadian runner named Ben Johnson won a gold medal in the 100 meter dash, but it was discovered that he was using steroids.

Johnson was disgraced, and the gold medal was given to Carl Lewis, an American sprinter.

What is WADA?

After the Ben Johnson scandal, the IOC became much more serious about drug testing, and in 1999, they created a new organization called the World Anti-Doping Agency (WADA).

WADA was created so that there could be one organization with one set of rules to control all of the various Olympic sports in many different countries. Each country and each sport still tests its athletes, but WADA makes the rules now.

Another big change is that in the past, athletes were usually only tested during the Olympics. Athletes often cheat by using PEDs in cycles, and they stop taking them just before the Olympics, so it is difficult to detect the PEDs in tests.

Now, WADA rules say that athletes have to be tested at other times as well. Because of this, it is becoming more difficult to cheat.

In recent years, fewer athletes have been caught using PEDs. However, no one knows if it is because fewer athletes are using them, or if it is because people are getting better at cheating.

How much do the Olympics cost?

It is very, very expensive to host the Olympic Games. Of course, the cost of every Olympics is different. It depends on the city and the country, and many other things.

No one knows exactly how much was spent, but many people say that the 2008 Olympics in Beijing cost over $20 billion. The city had to build a new subway system, an airport terminal, and many other public facilities.

Olympic flame in Vancouver, Canada *(photo: Marilyn Burgess)*

The Winter Olympics are usually cheaper. It is thought that the 2010 Winter Olympics in Vancouver, Canada, cost seven or eight billion dollars.

Before the Olympic Games, some people always complain about the cost. They think that it is almost impossible to make money from the Olympics. Cities often spend a lot of money to build stadiums and other buildings that are never used again, and the people often have to pay higher taxes.

It does cost a lot of money to hold the Olympics, but many cities think that they are good for the economy. They believe that it will help the city to make much more money from tourism, Olympic sponsors, and money paid by TV stations. If the Olympics are successful, it is said that a city can get back billions of dollars.

Why were there no women in the first Olympics?

When the Olympics started in 1896, women were treated very differently than they are today. In those days, many people believed that women were too weak to compete in sports. They did not think that women should have jobs, and the same kind of thinking made them think that women did not belong in the Olympics either.

People in those days also thought that it was wrong for women to wear clothes that showed their bodies, so it was especially difficult to compete in events like swimming.

Sadly, Pierre de Coubertin also believed these things and said that the only thing women should do in sports was to encourage their sons to play them.

Because of these ways of thinking, it took a

long time for women to be able to compete in the Olympics the same way that men do.

When did women start competing in the Olympics?

The first women competed in the 1900 Olympics in Paris, France, but they were in only two events: lawn tennis and golf. The first woman ever to win an Olympic championship was Charlotte Cooper. She was British, and she was also a great champion at Wimbledon.

In 1912, women were allowed to compete in swimming events, and in 1928, they were first allowed to compete in track and field. However, people believed that longer distance events like the 800 meter race were too dangerous for women.

During the 1928 Olympics, there were many shocking news stories about the 800 meter running race. Reporters said that five of the eleven runners could not finish the

Women's tennis tournament at the 1900 Olympic Games

race, and that another five collapsed after it. This story became famous all over the world, and it made many people think that women should not compete in track and field. But the story was not true.

The real story is that all of the women finished the race, and a German woman named Lina Radke set a new world record. It was true that some of the women lay down to rest after the race, but they did not "collapse." Because of the untrue story, women were not allowed to run in any races longer than 200 meters until the year 1960!

It took a long time, but people finally began to learn that women can play any sport that men can play, and today some of the greatest Olympic champions are women.

How did the Winter Olympics begin?

When the Summer Olympics started, the IOC did not think that it was necessary to have a Winter Olympics. They wanted only sports that are played all over the world to be played in the Olympics.

The sports in the Winter Olympics are usually only played in countries that have a lot of snow, so the IOC did not think that it was necessary to have them in the Olympics. They also thought that countries with a lot of snow would have an unfair advantage in the Winter Olympics.

However, many people wanted to see winter sports such as figure skating and skiing in the Olympics. In the 1908 Olympics in London, England, figure skating was a demonstration sport, and the 1920 Olympics in Antwerp, Belgium, had both figure skating and ice hockey.

These events were very successful, and the IOC finally decided to start an "International Sports Week" in 1924. More than 250 athletes from 16 countries came to Chamonix, France, for this event. It was very successful, and it was later decided that this was the first Winter Olympics.

In those days, it was difficult for athletes to

travel to cold countries for training, so athletes from countries such as Finland and Norway had a big advantage. These two countries won 28 medals, more than all the rest of the countries together.

An American man named Charles Jewtraw won the first gold medal in the Winter Olympics in the 500 meter speed skating event.

After the International Sports Week in 1924, the Winter Olympics began to be held every four years. More sports were added, and in the 2010 Vancouver Olympics, there were 15 sports and 86 different events.

What is the "Olympic village"?

When over 10,000 athletes from 200 different countries come to compete in the Olympics, they all need a safe, comfortable place to stay. They need a place where they can get a good night's sleep and healthy meals without being bothered by fans and journalists. The place where the athletes stay is called the Olympic village, and being there can be an amazing experience.

Olympic athletes say that the Olympic village is like another world. Almost everyone there is an athlete or coach, and the people are thinking about only one thing: winning an Olympic medal.

Everyone in the Olympic village has a huge amount of energy, and there is a feeling of excitement there that cannot be experienced anywhere else.

Athletes say that it is amazing to walk around in the Olympic village and see large numbers of great athletes who have won medals in past Olympics, and to be able to talk to them or even sit at the same table with them during meals.

It can also be very surprising to see dozens of people walking around wearing gold, silver, or bronze medals. Many winners are so excited about their medals that they wear them for days after their event has ended, and some even sleep with them!

How many people watch the Olympics around the world?

The Olympics are watched by more people than any other TV program or sporting event in the world. Almost four billion people around the world watched the 2008 Olympics in Beijing! It is said that almost 80 percent of people who live in places with electricity watch the Summer Olympics.

In the United States, a survey during the 2010 Winter Olympics found that 46 percent of Olympic viewers changed their daily schedules to watch the Olympics. About 66 percent cheered aloud while watching, and 35 percent of them cried at least once!

What happens during the opening and closing ceremonies?

The opening ceremonies at the Olympic Games are one of the most amazing events in the world. Every Olympic Games has a different ceremony, but there are some things that always happen:

The greeting and parade ....

First, the president of the IOC greets the country's head of state. After that, there is a parade of athletes. All of the athletes march together with the other members of their country's team. All of the teams enter the stadium in alphabetical order, except the Greek team and the team from the host country. The Greeks are always first, and the team from the host country is always last.

The opening ....

After the parade, the president of the IOC introduces the country's head of state. The head of state makes a speech and says that the Olympics have begun. Then, the Olympic flag is carried into the stadium and raised.

Opening Ceremonies of the 2010 Olympic Games

The oath

Another important event is the Olympic oath. Each country chooses one person who will carry the country's flag, and these people all stand in a circle. Then, one athlete, one judge, and one coach from the host nation stand in the center. They each hold a corner of a large Olympic flag in their left hand, raise their right hand, and promise to compete or judge in a way that follows the rules of their sport.

The lighting of the flame

The most exciting moment of the opening ceremonies is usually the lighting of the Olympic flame. This is the end of the long torch relay that began in Olympia, Greece.

The last runner finally enters the stadium. He or she then gives the torch to the person who will light the flame. The person who lights the flame is usually someone who is very famous, important, or a symbol of the country. For example, during the 1964 Summer Olympics in Tokyo, Japan, a man named Yoshinori Sakai lit the Olympic flame. He was not an Olympic athlete, but he was born in the city of Hiroshima on the day the atomic bomb was dropped. He symbolized the rebirth of Japan after World War II.

During the 1996 Olympics in Atlanta, in the United States, the flame was lit by the famous boxer Muhammad Ali. Not only was Ali an Olympic champion (He won a gold medal during the 1960 Summer Olympics in Rome, Italy.), but he was suffering from Parkinson's Disease.

This terrible disease makes it difficult for people to walk and causes their bodies to shake. When Ali lit the Olympic flame, he moved very slowly, and everyone could see that it was very difficult for him to hold the torch. But everyone watching was moved by Ali's great courage and dignity.

How much money are Olympic medals worth?

The medals are different at every Olympics,

so their value is always different. The IOC has some rules about the materials and designs for the medals, but the sizes and symbols on them are chosen by the host country.

Olympic medals seem to be getting bigger and bigger these days. The ones at the 1994 Winter Olympics in Lillehammer, Norway, were only about 130 grams, but the medals at the 2010 Winter Olympics in Vancouver, Canada, were the largest in history. They were 100 millimeters in diameter, and they weighed about half a kilogram.

Gold and silver prices are always changing, but at the time of the Vancouver Olympics, the gold medals (which were actually silver with gold plate on the outside) were worth about $500, and silver medals were about half of that. Bronze is very cheap, so they would be worth just a few dollars.

What are demonstration sports?

For many years, the Olympics had special sports

called "demonstration sports." These sports were played during the Olympics, but they were not official Olympic sports.

Usually, demonstration sports were sports that were very popular in the host country. For example, during the 1988 Summer Olympics in Seoul, South Korea, tae kwon do was a demonstration sport, and in 1984, baseball was a demonstration sport at the Los Angeles Summer Olympics in the United States.

The purpose of demonstration sports was to show sports that were an important part of the host country's culture. They were also a good chance to promote these sports because people around the world were watching the Olympics. Sometimes demonstration sports became official Olympic sports if they were very popular.

In 1992, however, the IOC decided that there will not be any more demonstration sports. This was because there are so many regular sports that there is not time for demonstration sports.

What is a "boycott"?

Sometimes countries decide that they will not send athletes to the Olympics, because they want to protest something. For example, when the Soviet Union attacked the country of Afghanistan in 1979, the United States became very angry.

When Russia held the Olympics the next year, America decided that they would not send any athletes to the Games. Sixty-four other countries joined America and decided that they would boycott the Olympics too.

Four years later, when the Olympics were held in Los Angeles, California, the Soviet Union decided that it would not send any athletes to America. It was joined by 14 other countries.

There have been five different Olympic Games in which some countries did not send athletes, for political reasons.

During a boycott, the country's leaders feel that it is very important for the athletes from their countries to stay home during an Olympics. However, it is always very difficult for the athletes themselves. They have trained for years and years for the Olympics.

Even worse, the Olympics are held only once every four years, so many of the athletes know that they will be too old to compete at the next Olympic Games.

The Olympics are supposed to be an event where politics are not important, so it is always very sad when a country feels that it cannot send athletes to them.

Have the Olympics ever been affected by terrorism?

One of the most important goals of the Olympics is to help to bring peace to the world. Sadly, however, there are terrorists who think that if they hurt or kill people during the Olympics, the world will listen to their message or give them the things they want.

During the 1972 Summer Olympics in Munich, West Germany, a terrorist group called

Black September kidnapped nine members of the Israeli Olympic team.

The terrorists were Palestinians, and they wanted Israel to release Palestinian prisoners from jail. The German police tried to rescue the Israelis, but all nine were killed.

The terrorist attack at the Munich Olympics shocked the world, and it changed the Olympics forever.

Now, host countries have to spend millions of dollars on security, the athletes cannot come and go freely from the Olympic village, and soldiers are everywhere during the Games.

However, the IOC hopes that someday the Olympics' message of peace will spread around the world and that athletes will be able to come together without worrying about terrorism.

Plaque for atheletes killed during the 1972 Summer Olympics
(photo: Andreas Thum)

Can disabled people compete in the regular Olympics?

The Olympic Games are open to anyone who qualifies for them. Any disabled athlete can compete if he or she is good enough.

There is an Olympics called the Paralympics for disabled people, but sometimes they also compete in the regular Olympics.

For example, a man named George Eyser won an amazing six medals in one day during the 1904 Olympics in St. Louis, in the United States. He won three gold medals, two silver medals, and one bronze medal in gymnastics events.

His performance would have been amazing for a normal athlete, but Eyser had only one leg! The 1904 Olympics had fewer athletes than normal, but it was still an incredible performance.

There have been many other disabled Olympic athletes in the past hundred years, and sometimes they are able to compete with the best athletes in the world.

At the 1988 Summer Olympics in Seoul,

South Korea, an American pitcher with no right hand named Jim Abbot helped his team win a gold medal.

During the 2000 Summer Olympics in Sydney, Australia, a blind American woman named Marla Runyan finished eighth in the 1,500 meter race.

At the 2008 Summer Olympics in Beijing, China, Natalie du Toit from South Africa competed in the 10 kilometer swimming event even though she has only one leg.

What are the Paralympics?

The Paralympics are like the Olympic Games, but they are for disabled athletes. The name comes from the Greek words "para" and "Olympics." "Para" means "beside," so "Paralympics" means an Olympics that is held along with the main Olympics.

The Paralympics are held every four years, and they are always in the same city that hosts the Olympics. They are usually held a few weeks after the Olympics have finished, and they usually use the same stadiums and buildings as the Olympics. The Paralympics' motto is "Spirit in motion."

The Paralympics are not as famous as some other sporting events, but they are the second-largest sporting event in the world, after the Olympics. Disabled athletes come from all over the world to compete in them.

More than 4,200 athletes from 148 countries came to Beijing, China, for the 2008 Paralympics.

The Paralympics started in 1948. They were held in London, England, and were started by a doctor named Ludwig Guttmann. He worked at a hospital for soldiers who had been badly hurt during World War II, and he thought that the Paralympics would be a good way to improve their health and self-respect.

At first, the Paralympics were only for British soldiers who had been injured in World War II. The games began to grow quickly, however, and in 1960, people who had not been soldiers were invited to join. They began using the same stadiums and buildings as the Olympics in 1988. The Summer Paralympics have 20 sports, and the Winter Paralympics have 5.

Many of the sports, such as weightlifting, archery, judo, and tennis, are the same as at the Olympics. However, the athletes usually compete in wheelchairs or use other special equipment to help them.

Today, the Paralympics is full of elite athletes who play their sports at the highest level. The Paralympics is an inspiration to millions of people around the world. It shows them that with hard work and a strong spirit, disabled people can lead useful and active lives.

What are the Youth Olympic Games?

The Youth Olympic Games are a special Olympics that are held for young people between the ages of 14 and 18. They were first held in the year 2010 in Singapore. Like the Olympics, they are held every four years, and there are both summer and winter versions.

An Austrian man named Johann Rosenzopf first had the idea for the Youth Olympic Games in 1998. He was worried because young people around the world seemed to be spending less time playing sports and because they seemed to be getting fatter.

Rosenzopf also thought that the Youth Olympic Games would be good training for young people who might someday compete in the Olympics. They would give young athletes a chance to experience a high-level international competition.

More than 3,600 athletes from over 200 countries competed in the first 2010 Youth

Opening ceremonies of the 2010 Youth Olympic Games in Singapore
(photo: Walter Lim)

Olympic Games, and they were a big success.

Most of the events are similar to Olympic events, but sometimes they are changed a little so that they will be easier or safer for young athletes. For example, the basketball teams have only three players instead of five, and the games are played on half the court, with periods of five minutes each.

During the games, the athletes often have a chance to meet famous Olympic athletes, and there are classes on things like health and fitness, the environment, and career planning.

The Youth Olympics are a high-level sports competition, but they are also an event that hopes to make young people healthier and teach them to be useful members of society.

Part 3
Medals, Records, and Athletes

Who is the greatest Olympic athlete of all time?

There have been so many great Olympic athletes that it is impossible to choose just one as the greatest. Here are three that many people think are amazing.

Nadia Comaneci

Before the 1976 Summer Olympics in Montreal, Canada, no one thought that it was possible to score a perfect ten in gymnastics. In fact, the scoreboards could only show scores of 9.99

Part 3 Medals, Records, and Athletes

Nadia Comaneci
(photo: Dave Gilbert)

or lower. But then a gymnast from Romania did a perfect routine and shocked the world.

Nadia Comaneci was only 14 years old, and she was very small. She was just 150 centimeters tall, and she weighed just 39 kilograms. When people saw her do her routines, no one could believe that such a young girl could do so many amazing things. She did all her moves perfectly, and she did new moves that no one had ever seen before.

Comaneci's first routine was on the uneven bars. She flew through the air in a way that no one could believe. She moved with incredible speed, but she was always in total control, and she was as graceful as a dancer. When she finished, the arena was totally silent. No one could believe what they had seen. The scoreboards had to show her score as 1.0, but of course it was a ten.

After that, Comaneci won six more events with perfect tens. She won three gold medals, a silver, and a bronze.

Michael Phelps..................

Michael Phelps is one of the greatest swimmers of all time, and he has won more gold medals at the Olympics than any other athlete. He won six gold and two bronze medals at the 2004 Summer Olympics in Athens, Greece, and then at the 2008 Summer Olympics in Beijing, China, he won eight gold medals.

Of course, Phelps is a very talented athlete, but many people say that the reason he was able to win so many gold medals is that he works harder than anyone else. He trained every day for five years without a single day off, even swimming on Christmas day. During some of his workouts, he swam 10,000 meters or more. It takes him about two and a half

Michael Phelps

hours to swim 10,000 meters, and he was swimming as fast as he could for the whole time.

During the Beijing Olympics, Phelps had to swim 17 times in 9 days if he wanted to win 8 gold medals. It was a tough schedule that many people thought was impossible. But Phelps won, and won, and won again. After his sixth gold medal, Phelps thought he was too tired to win any more. But he kept trying, and in the seventh race, he won by just one one-hundredth of a second. It was a superhuman effort.

The eighth and final race was the 4 × 100 meter relay. The United States was racing against Japan and Australia, two very tough swimming teams. When Phelps jumped into the pool as the third of four swimmers, the United States team was behind both of them. But thanks to his years of hard work, he was able to bring his team into first place. The fourth man on the team also swam well, and Phelps got his eighth gold medal.

Not only did Phelps win eight gold medals in one Olympics, but he set seven world records and eight Olympic records while doing it. Phelps may be the greatest swimmer of all time. As of December 19, 2009, he had 39 world records.

Carl Lewis

Many people say that Carl Lewis is the greatest Olympic champion in history because of the many gold medals that he won and because of his long career.

Lewis first became famous during the 1984 Summer Olympics in Los Angeles, in the United States. He won gold medals in the 100 meter sprint, the long jump, the 200 meter sprint, and the 4 × 100 meter relay. He was such a great athlete that after the 1984 Olympics, Lewis was invited to join professional basketball and football teams, but he decided to continue doing track and field.

Staying in track and field was the right choice for Lewis because he won more medals

Carl Lewis

in the 1988 Summer Olympics in Seoul, South Korea. He won gold in the 100 meter sprint and set a world record at the same time. He also won another gold medal in the long jump and a silver in the 200 meter sprint.

Most track and field athletes are lucky to be able to compete in just one Olympics, but at the 1992 Summer Olympics in Barcelona, Spain, Lewis competed in his third. He won another gold medal in the long jump, and then got one more in the 4 × 100 meter relay.

No one thought that Carl Lewis would be able to compete in the 1996 Summer Olympics in Atlanta, in the United States. He was 35 years old, and there were a lot of very young, strong athletes on the American team. However, not only was Lewis chosen for the team, but he was able to win another gold medal in the long jump.

In 1999, Carl Lewis was named the "Sportsman of the Century" by the IOC, and *Sports Illustrated* magazine called him the "Olympian of the Century."

What country has won the most Olympic medals?

The United States has won more medals than any other country. Since 1896, Americans have won 2,296 medals in the Summer Olympics and 253 in the Winter Olympics. That is a total of 2,549 medals.

The Soviet Union is not a country anymore, but it won 1,010 medals in the Summer Olympics and 194 in the Winter Olympics, for a total of 1,204.

Germany won 851 medals in the Summer Olympics and 248 in the Winter Olympics, for a total of 1099.

Other countries in the top ten are Great Britain (737 in total), France (730 in total), Italy (627 in total), Sweden (604 in total), the former East Germany (519 in total), Hungary (465 in total), and Finland (455 in total).

Have any athletes ever won medals at both the Winter and Summer Olympics?

Only four athletes have ever won medals in both

the Summer and Winter Olympics. At the 1920 Summer Olympics in Antwerp, Belgium, a man named Eddie Eagan won a gold medal in boxing. Twelve years later, at the 1932 Winter Olympics in Lake Placid, in the United States, he won another gold medal in the four-men bobsled event.

Eddie Eagan

The only athlete who has ever won a medal at both the Summer and Winter Olympics in the same year is a woman named Christa Luding-Rothenburger. She is from Germany, and she was one of the best speed skaters in the world for more than 10 years in the 1980s.

In 1980, Luding-Rothenburger's coach recommended that she start cycling as well. She quickly became an excellent cyclist, and at the 1988 Winter Olympics in Calgary, Canada, she won a gold medal in the 1,000 meter speed skating event and a silver in the 500 meters. Seven months later, she won a silver medal in the 1,000 meter sprint in cycling at the Summer Olympics in Seoul, South Korea.

Has any athlete ever set a world record without winning a gold medal?

In most sports, if you set a world record, you will win a gold medal. The pentathlon, however, has five different events, so it is possible to set a world record without winning a medal.

During the 1924 Olympics in Paris, France, an athlete named Robert LeGendre from America jumped 7.76 meters and set a world record in the long jump. However, he did not do so well in the other events and finished third, winning a bronze medal.

Who were some of the toughest athletes ever?

Of course, an athlete has to be very tough to get to the Olympics, but there have also been some athletes who have been able to win their events even though they were badly injured while competing. One of the most famous of these is the Japanese gymnast Shun Fujimoto, and many people say that he is the toughest ever.

Fujimoto competed in the 1976 Summer

Olympics in Montreal, Canada, when most people expected that the team from the Soviet Union would win the gold medal. However, the Japanese team was also very strong, so the competition was very close.

Both teams were giving excellent performances, but then during his routine in the floor exercise, Fujimoto hurt his knee. It was very painful, and everyone thought that he would have to quit. However, the Japanese team knew that if he continued to compete, they would have a chance to beat the Russians. Everyone in Japan wanted them to win a gold medal, and Fujimoto decided to continue.

Fujimoto realized that his knee was broken, but he decided not to tell anyone because he had two more events to finish. After the floor exercises, he had to do the pommel horse. Although he was in terrible pain, he got a score of 9.5 out of 10.

The last event was the rings. Fujimoto knew that at the end of this event, he would have to jump into the air and land on his broken leg. But he decided that he could not give up.

The score was very close, and if Fujimoto's routine was good enough, Japan had a good chance to beat the Soviet Union.

Before Fujimoto started, his face was gray and he was covered with sweat. People knew there was something wrong, but no one knew his knee was broken. During his routine, Fujimoto was in terrible pain, but he did not give up. He did an excellent routine with only very tiny mistakes.

Finally, he somersaulted backwards twice through the air and landed perfectly. He stood without moving for a few seconds, and then fell to the ground in the worst pain of his life.

The Japanese team won the gold medal, and Fujimoto became an Olympic legend.

Which athletes have competed in the most games?

The Olympic Games are held only once every four years, and athletes are usually at the peak of their abilities when they are young. For this reason, many great athletes only get a chance to compete in one or two Olympic Games at the most. But there are some athletes who are able to continue competing at a very high level for years and years.

For example, Hubert Raudaschl of Austria competed in nine Olympics between 1964 and 1996. During his 36 years of competing, he won two silver medals in the sailing competition.

A Canadian man named Ian Millar has also competed in nine Olympic Games. He competes in the equestrian competition, and won a silver medal.

Although Raudaschl and Millar are great Olympians, you do not need to be strong or fast to win medals in their events. Athletes such as Seiko Hashimoto from Japan, Merlene Ottey, who competed for both Jamaica and Slovenia, and Jeannie Longo from France have all competed in seven Olympic Games, and they all do sports that need a lot of speed and muscle power.

Seiko Hashimoto competes in both the

Summer and Winter Olympics, and she does both speed skating and cycling, so she was able to go to seven Olympic Games in just 12 years. She won a bronze medal at the Winter Olympics in Albertville, France, in 1992.

Merlene Ottey competes in track and field, and she has won nine Olympic medals over a period of 24 years. Jeannie Longo is one of the greatest cycling champions of all time, and she won a gold medal, two silver medals, and a bronze medal during her 24 years as an Olympic athlete.

Merlene Ottey

Who was the oldest athlete ever to win a gold medal?

Oscar Swahn, a Swedish Olympic athlete, won a shooting event at the 1912 Olympics in Stockholm, Sweden. Eight years later, he became the oldest person to ever win a medal at the Olympics when he got a silver in the same event at the 1920 Olympics in Antwerp, Belgium. He was 72 years old.

Who was the youngest athlete ever to win an Olympic event?

No one knows the name of the youngest person ever to win an event at the Olympics, but we do know that he was between seven and ten years old.

In the 1900 Olympics, the Dutch rowing team was worried that one of their members was too heavy. They decided to replace him and asked a young French boy to go with them in their boat. The boy knew nothing about rowing, but he was very light, and the Dutch team won.

The young French boy was very shy, and he snuck away after the race. He probably did not receive a medal, but he did help the Dutch win.

The youngest person ever to receive an individual gold medal at the Olympics is Tara Lipinski. She won the Ladies' Singles gold medal in figure skating at the 1998 Winter Olympics in Nagano, Japan. She was just 15 years old.

What are some of the most famous Olympic records?

There have been many record-breaking

performances at the Olympics, but most people agree that the greatest was Bob Beamon's long jump at the 1968 Summer Olympics in Mexico City, Mexico.

When a new Olympic record is set, an athlete usually runs a tenth of a second faster or jumps a centimeter or two farther. But Bob Beamon's jump was more than half a meter longer than the old record.

On October 18, 1968, he jumped an incredible 8.90 meters. The other athletes could not believe what Beamon had done. A famous Soviet jumper named Igor Ter-Ovanesyan said, "Compared to this jump, we are as children," and Lynn Davies, the gold medal winner from the 1964 Olympics said, "You have destroyed this event."

Another amazing record was set by Emil Zatopek. During the 1952 Summer Olympics in Helsinki, Finland, he won both the 5,000 meter and 10,000 meter races. He decided to enter the marathon as well, even though he had never run in one before. For the first half of the race,

Part 3 Medals, Records, and Athletes

he ran behind a famous British runner named Jim Peters. But halfway through the race, Zatopek asked him, "The pace? Is it good enough?"

Peters told him it was too slow, and Zatopek began to run more quickly.

Emil Zatopek
(photo: Deutsche Fotothek)

When he finished the race, he was two and a half minutes faster than the old Olympic record. No one could believe that it was possible to win three tough races in such a short time.

A third amazing record was set by Usain Bolt during the 2008 Summer Olympics in Beijing, China. He ran in the 100 meter race, and this event is very difficult to set a new record in. The athletes in this event are now running in less than 10 seconds, and sometimes it seems impossible for a human body to move any faster. But near the end of the race, Bolt was so far ahead of the other runners that he slowed down and raised his arms to celebrate before he reached the finish line. Not only that, but one of his shoelaces was untied.

Bolt's new world record was 9.86 seconds. A few days later, he also set a world record in the 200 meters and became the first person to set world records in both these events during the same Olympics.

What were some of the most emotional moments in the Olympics?

The Olympics are not just a sporting competition. They are filled with human drama as well. Here are two incredible moments that moved many people who watched them:

Derek Redmond's fall ....

Many people will never forget the story of Derek Redmond during the 1992 Summer Olympics in Barcelona, Spain. Derek Redmond was one of the fastest runners in the world, and many people expected that he would get a gold medal in the men's 400 meter race. However, during one of the qualifying races, something terrible happened.

When he was just over halfway finished the race, Redmond hurt his leg very badly. He fell down, and a medical team came to carry Redmond off the track, but he refused to be carried on a stretcher because he wanted to finish the race. His dream of an Olympic gold medal was over, but he decided not to quit.

Derek Redmond
(photo: Parliament Speakers Limited)

Redmond quickly stood up and began hobbling toward the finish line, but he was in terrible pain. His father was in the stadium to watch his son run, and he knew that he had to do something.

Only a few people are allowed near the track during a race, but no one could stop Redmond's father from going to help his son. He ran down onto the track and said to his son, "We'll finish together."

The race was over, but the crowd began to cheer again. Redmond's father put his arm around him, and the two men began slowly moving toward the finish line.

Just before the finish line, Redmond's father let go of him so that he could finish the race by himself. Redmond crossed the finish line, and the two men hugged each other, crying. Redmond and his father were not the only ones crying that day. Thousands more people in the stadium also cried when they say Redmond's bravery and his father's great love for his son.

Lawrence Lemieux's rescue ....

Lawrence Lemieux was another man who did not win his event, but moved the hearts of many people. Lemieux was a Canadian sailor competing in the 1988 Olympics in Seoul, South Korea.

Lemieux was in second place and seemed very likely to get a silver medal. However, the weather suddenly became very windy, and Lemieux saw two Singaporean sailors from another race fall into the water. Both of the men were hurt and could not get back into their boat.

It was obvious what Lemieux had to do. He

quickly changed direction and began sailing toward the two Singaporean sailors. He helped them to get into his small boat, even though it was dangerous to have more than one person in it, and they waited for someone to come and rescue them.

Lemieux lost his chance to win a normal medal, but he got one that may be more special. Over the years, hundreds of athletes have received gold, silver, and bronze medals, but only nine people have gotten another medal called the Pierre de Coubertin medal. It is a special medal given to athletes who show the Olympic spirit of sportsmanship that was so important to Pierre de Coubertin.

Lemieux was given the medal because he was helping people that he had never met before, two men from another country who were competing in a different sport from him. He was at the Olympics to win a medal for himself and his country, but he gave everything up to help others. On that day, Lawrence Lemieux truly showed the spirit of the modern Olympic Games.

Word List

- 本文で使われている全ての語を掲載しています（LEVEL 1、2）。ただし、LEVEL 3 以上は、中学校レベルの語を含みません。
- 語形が規則変化する語の見出しは原形で示しています。不規則変化語は本文中で使われている形になっています。
- 一般的な意味を紹介していますので、一部の語で本文で実際に使われている品詞や意味と合っていないことがあります。
- 品詞は以下のように示しています。

名 名詞	代 代名詞	形 形容詞	副 副詞	動 動詞	助 助動詞
前 前置詞	接 接続詞	間 間投詞	冠 冠詞	略 略語	俗 俗語
頭 接頭語	尾 接尾語	記 記号	関 関係代名詞		

A

- □ **a ~ or two** 1〜か2〜, 2, 3の
- □ **ability** 名 能力, 才能
- □ **about to** 《be –》まさに〜しようとしている, 〜するところだ
- □ **accept** 動 ①受け入れる ②認める
- □ **accident** 名 (不慮の)事故, 災難
- □ **active** 形 活動的な
- □ **actually** 副 実際には, 実は
- □ **AD** 西暦〜年
- □ **advantage** 名 有利な点［立場］, 強み, 優越
- □ **affect** 動 影響する
- □ **Afghanistan** 名 アフガニスタン《国》
- □ **Africa** 名 アフリカ《大陸》
- □ **after a while** しばらくして
- □ **agon** 名 懸賞付きの競技
- □ **ahead of** 〜より先［前］に, 〜に先んじて
- □ **airplane** 名 飛行機
- □ **Albertville** 名 アルベールビル《フランスの都市, 1992年冬季オリンピック開催地》
- □ **alcohol** 名 アルコール
- □ **Ali, Muhammad** (モハメド・)アリ《ボクサー, アメリカ。1960年ローマオリンピック・ライトヘビー級金メダリスト。史上初めてWBAヘビー級王座を三度獲得した》
- □ **all** 熟 all kinds of さまざまな, あらゆる種類の all the others 他の全員を all the time いつも all the way ずっと
- □ **allow** 動 許す, 《– … to 〜》…が〜するのを可能にする, …に〜させておく
- □ **along with** 〜と一緒に
- □ **aloud** 副 大声で, (聞こえるように)声を出して
- □ **alphabetical** 形 アルファベット順の, ABC順の
- □ **also** 熟 A but also B Aだけでなく また B も
- □ **although** 接 〜だけれども, 〜にもかかわらず, たとえ〜でも
- □ **altius** より高く《ラテン語, オリンピックのスローガンである, より速くより高くより強くの一つ》
- □ **aluminum** 名 アルミニウム
- □ **always** 熟 not always 必ずしも〜であるとは限らない
- □ **amateur** 名 アマチュア, スポーツ

Word List

をすることが職業ではない人
- **amateurism** 名 アマチュアリズム《オリンピック出場選手は,スポーツを職業とし,スポーツをすることで報酬を得る人々であってはならないとする考え方》
- **amazing** 形 驚くべき,見事な
- **America** 名 アメリカ《国名・大陸》
- **American** 形 アメリカ(人)の 名 アメリカ人
- **amount** 名 量
- **amphetamine** 名 アンフェタミン《覚せい剤の一種》
- **Amsterdam** 名 アムステルダム《オランダの首都,1928年夏季オリンピック開催地》
- **anatomy** 名 生態構造,解剖学
- **ancient** 形 昔の,古代の
- **announce** 動 (人に)知らせる,公表する
- **another** 熟 one another お互い
- **Antwerp** 名 アントワープ《ベルギーの都市,1920年夏季オリンピック開催地》
- **anymore** 副 今はもう
- **anyone** 代 ①《否定文で》誰も(〜ない) ②《肯定文で》誰でも
- **anything else** ほかの何か
- **anywhere** 副 どこにも
- **Apollo** 名 アポロン《ギリシア神話の太陽神》
- **archaeologist** 名 考古学者
- **archery** 名 弓術,アーチェリー
- **arena** 名 競技場,アリーナ
- **armor** 名 よろい,甲冑 suits of armor よろい一式
- **artist** 名 芸術家
- **as** 熟 as 〜 as one can できる限り〜 as well なお,その上,同様に
- **Asia** 名 アジア
- **at** 熟 at the time そのころ,当時は

not 〜 at all 全く〜ではない
- **Athens** 名 アテネ《ギリシアの首都,1896年第一回オリンピック,2004年夏季オリンピック開催地》
- **athlete** 名 運動選手
- **athletic** 形 運動競技の
- **Atlanta** 名 アトランタ《アメリカの都市,1996年夏季オリンピック(近代オリンピック100周年記念大会)開催地》
- **atmosphere** 名 雰囲気
- **atomic bomb** 原子力爆弾
- **attack** 動 侵攻する,攻める 名 攻撃
- **attraction** 名 呼び物,アトラクション tourist attraction 観光名所
- **Australia** 名 オーストラリア《国名》
- **Australian** 形 オーストラリアの 名 オーストラリア人
- **Austria** 名 オーストリア《国名》
- **Austrian** 形 オーストリアの 名 オーストリア人
- **away** 熟 go away 治る stay away from 〜から離れている

B

- **back** 熟 bring back 戻す,呼び戻す get back 戻る,取り戻す
- **backwards** 副 後ろ向きに
- **badly** 副 とても,ひどく
- **ban** 動 禁止する
- **Barcelona** 名 バルセロナ《スペインの都市,1992年夏季オリンピック開催地》
- **base** 動 《- on 〜》〜に基礎を置く,基づく
- **baseball** 名 野球
- **basketball** 名 バスケットボール
- **battle** 名 戦闘,戦い

- **BC** 紀元前〜年
- **beat** 動打ち負かす
- **beauty** 名美, 美しい人
- **beginning** 名初め, 始まり
- **behave** 動振る舞う
- **behind** 前〜に遅れて, 〜に劣って 副後ろに, 背後に
- **Beijing** 名北京《中国の首都, 2008年夏期オリンピック開催地》
- **Belgium** 名ベルギー《国名》
- **believe in** 〜を信じる
- **belong** 動属する, 一員である
- **Ben Johnson** ベン・ジョンソン《陸上選手, カナダ。1988年に金メダルを獲るが, 薬物使用の発覚により剥奪される》
- **Berlin** 名ベルリン《ドイツの首都, 1936年夏季オリンピック開催地。1916年夏季オリンピック開催予定地でもあったが, 第一次世界大戦の影響を受けて中止された》
- **beside** 前〜のそばに, 〜と並んで
- **better** 熟 get better (病気などが) 良くなる
- **between A and B** AとBの間に
- **biathlon** 名バイアスロン《クロスカントリースキーと射撃を組み合わせた冬季の種目》
- **billion** 形10億の, ばく大な, 無数の 名10億
- **Black September** 黒い九月, ブラックセプテンバー《パレスチナの過激派組織》
- **blind** 形視覚障害がある, 目の不自由な
- **blow** 動 (風が) 吹く
- **Bob Beamon** ボブ・ビーモン《男子陸上走り幅跳び選手, アメリカ。1968年世界新記録で金メダルを獲得》
- **bobsled** 名ボブスレー《二人または四人乗りの専用のそりに乗ってコースを滑走し, タイムを競う冬季の種目》
- **bone** 名骨
- **Bosnia and Herzegovina** ボスニア・ヘルツェゴビナ《旧ユーゴスラビア, バルカン半島西部に位置する共和制国家》
- **both A and B** AもBも
- **both of them** 彼ら[それら]両方とも
- **bother** 動悩ます, 困惑させる
- **boxer** 名拳闘家, ボクシングの選手
- **boxing** 名ボクシング
- **boycott** 名ボイコット, 集団排斥, 一致して出席を放棄すること 動ボイコットする, 集団排斥をする
- **branch** 名枝
- **bravery** 名勇敢さ, 勇気ある行動
- **Brazil** 名ブラジル《国》
- **bring back** 戻す, 呼び戻す
- **British** 形英国人の 名英国人
- **bronze** 名ブロンズ, 青銅
- **building** 名建物, 造物, ビル
- **bull** 名雄牛
- **bump** 動ぶつかる, ぶつける
- **bury** 動埋める, 覆い隠す

C

- **calf** 名子牛
- **Calgary** 名カルガリー《カナダの都市, 1988年冬季オリンピック開催地》
- **California** 名カリフォルニア《米国の州》
- **camp** 動野営する, キャンプする
- **campaign** 名キャンペーン (活動, 運動)
- **Canada** 名カナダ《国名》

Word List

- **Canadian** 形 カナダ(人)の
- **cancel** 動 取り消す, 中止する
- **capital** 形 首都の
- **career** 名 ①(生涯の・専門的な)職業 ②経歴, キャリア
- **Carl Lewis** カール・ルイス《陸上選手, アメリカ。1984年〜1996年の間に短距離走, リレー, 走り幅飛びなどで九つの金メダルと一つの銀メダルを獲得した》
- **carry 〜 off** 〜を運び去る
- **carry into** 〜の中に運び入れる
- **carry on** 持ち運ぶ
- **case** 熟 in that case もしそうなら
- **celebrate** 動 祝う, 喜びを表す
- **celebration** 名 祭事, 儀式
- **centimeter** 名 センチメートル《長さの単位》
- **ceremony** 名 式典, 儀式 opening ceremony 開会式
- **challenge** 名 挑戦
- **Chamonix** 名 シャモニー《フランスの都市, 1924年第一回冬季オリンピック開催地》
- **champion** 名 優勝者, チャンピオン
- **championship** 名 選手権(試合)
- **character** 名 個性, 特性, 人格
- **chariot** 名 古代ギリシアやローマで使われていた, 馬にひかせて走る二輪戦車
- **Charles Jewtraw** チャールズ・ジュートロー《スピードスケート選手, アメリカ。1924年金メダル獲得》
- **Charlotte Cooper** シャーロット・クーパー《テニス選手, イギリス。1900年に女子として史上初のオリンピック金メダルを獲得した》
- **charter** 名《C-》憲章, 重大で原則的なことにかんするきまり
- **cheat** 動 不正をする, ごまかす
- **China** 名 中国《国名》
- **choice** 名 選択
- **Christa Luding-Rothenburger** クリスタ・ルディンク=ローテンブルガー《自転車競技選手兼, スピードスケート選手, 旧東ドイツ。1988年に冬季と夏季の両方のオリンピックでメダルを獲得という史上初の快挙を成し遂げた》
- **Christian** 名 キリスト教徒, クリスチャン 形 キリスト(教)の
- **Christmas** 名 クリスマス
- **circle** 熟 in a circle 輪になって
- **citius** より速く《ラテン語, オリンピックのスローガンである, より速くより高くより強くの一つ》
- **closing** 形 閉会の
- **coach** 名 コーチ, 指導者
- **collapse** 動 (過労, 病気などで)倒れる
- **collection** 名 集めたもの
- **come and** 〜しに行く
- **come up** 浮上する, 上ってくる
- **comfortable** 形 快適な, 心地いい
- **committee** 名 委員会
- **common** 形 普通の, ありふれた
- **communism** 名 共産主義(体制)
- **communist** 形 共産主義の, 共産党の
- **compare** 動 比較する, 比べる
- **compete** 動 ①競争する ②(競技に)参加する
- **competition** 名 競技会, 競争, コンペ
- **complain** 動 不平[苦情]を言う, ぶつぶつ言う
- **conference** 名 (学校, スポーツクラブなどの)競技連盟
- **contest** 名 (〜を目指す)競争, 競技, コンテスト
- **continent** 名 大陸

The Olympic FAQ

- **control** 動 ①管理[支配]する ②抑制する, コントロールする 名 制御, 統制
- **cooking** 名 料理, クッキング
- **cooperate** 動 協力する, 一致団結する
- **copy** 動 まねる
- **Corinth** 名 コリント《ギリシアの都市, 古代においては商業と芸術の中心》
- **Coroibos** 名 コロイボス《古代ギリシアの陸上選手, 第一回古代オリンピックの優勝者》
- **Cortina d'Ampezzo** コルティーナ・ダンペッツォ《イタリアの都市, 1956年冬季オリンピック開催地》
- **cost** 名 費用, 値段 動 (金・費用が)かかる, (人に金額を)費やさせる
- **Coubertin** 名 (ピエール・ド・)クーベルタン《近代オリンピックの提唱, 創設者。1863-1937》
- **count** 動 数える
- **courage** 名 勇気, 度胸
- **court** 名 (スポーツの)コート
- **covered with** 熟《be –》～でおおわれている
- **crash** 名 激突事故
- **create** 動 創設する, 生み出す
- **cricket** 名 クリケット《野球に似た球技》
- **croquet** 名 クロッケー《ゲートボールの原型である球技》
- **crowd** 動 群がる, 殺到する 名 群集, 人混み
- **cycle** 名 周期 in cycles 周期的に反復して
- **cycling** 名 サイクリング, 自転車競技
- **cyclist** 名 自転車乗り, 自転車競技選手

D

- **daily** 形 毎日の, 日常の
- **dancer** 名 舞踏家, ダンサー
- **Dane** 名 デンマーク人
- **Danish** 形 デンマーク(人)の
- **dash** 名 短距離競争
- **day** 熟 in those days その当時は on that day その日 these days このごろ
- **decision** 名 決定
- **defeat** 名 敗北
- **degree** 名 (角度の)度
- **Delphi** 名 デルフォイ《古代ギリシアの都市》
- **demonstration** 名 デモンストレーション, 実演
- **demonstration sport** 公開競技《正式な種目ではなく, 見てもらうために行う競技》
- **depend on** ～をあてにする, ～しだいである
- **Derek Redmond** デレク・レドモンド《陸上選手, イギリス。1992年400メートル走の途中で肉離れを起こすが, 父に励まされながらゴールした》
- **design** 動 設計する, デザインする 名 デザイン, 設計
- **destroy** 動 破壊する, めちゃくちゃにする
- **detect** 動 見つける, 検出する
- **develop** 動 発達する[させる]
- **diameter** 名 直径
- **differently** 副 (～と)異なって, 違って
- **dignity** 名 威厳, 尊厳, 貫禄
- **direction** 名 方向, 方角
- **directly** 副 じかに, 直接に
- **dirty** 形 ①汚い, 汚れた ②卑劣な, 不正な
- **disabled** 形 身体障害のある

Word List

- **discipline** 名 科目, 分野
- **discus** 名 競技用の円盤
- **disease** 名 病気
- **disgrace** 動 しりぞける, 面目をつぶす
- **distance** 名 距離
- **diving** 名 水泳の飛び込み競技
- **document** 名 文書, 記録
- **dogsled** 名 犬ぞり
- **dolichos** 名 ドリコス走《古代オリンピックで行われていた長距離走》
- **doping** 名 ドーピング《スポーツで好成績をあげるために禁止された薬物を使用すること》
- **down** 熟 slow down 速度を落とす
- **dozens of people** 数十人もの人々, 多くの人々
- **dragon boat** ドラゴンボート《中国由来の細長く, 竜の装飾が施された船》
- **drama** 名 ①劇, 演劇 ②劇的なできごと
- **driver** 名 (馬車の)御者
- **drug** 名 薬, 薬物
- **Dutch** 形 オランダ(人)の

E

- **each other** お互いに
- **each time** 〜するたびに
- **Earth** 熟 everyone on Earth 誰でも, 全員
- **earthquake** 名 地震
- **easily** 副 円滑に, 容易に
- **economy** 名 経済
- **Eddie Eagan** エディー・イーガン《アメリカ。1920年にボクシングで, 1932年ボブスレーで金メダルを獲得, 夏季と冬季の両方のオリンピックで金メダルを獲得した史上初の人》
- **education** 名 教育, 教養
- **effect** 名 影響, 効果
- **effort** 名 努力(の成果)
- **Egypt** 名 エジプト《国名》
- **elect** 動 選挙で選ぶ
- **electricity** 名 電気
- **Elis** 名 エーリス《古代ギリシアの都市》
- **elite** 形 一流の, えり抜きの
- **else** any〜 else 他のあらゆる〜
- **embarrass** 動 恥ずかしい思いをさせる
- **embarrassing** 形 恥ずかしい, きまりが悪い
- **Emil Zatopek** エミール・ザトペック《陸上長距離走選手, チェコ。1952年に5000メートル, 10000メートル, マラソンで三つの金メダルを獲得する快挙をなしとげた》
- **emotional** 形 感動的な, 感情に訴える
- **emperor** 名 皇帝
- **empire** 名 帝国
- **encourage** 動 促進する, 奨励する
- **end** 熟 in the end 最後には, ついには
- **endurance** 名 持久力, 耐久力, スタミナ
- **enemy** 名 敵
- **England** 名 英国, イギリス
- **environment** 名 環境, 自然環境
- **equipment** 名 設備, 装備品, 用具
- **Europe** 名 ヨーロッパ
- **even though** 〜であるけれども, 〜にもかかわらず
- **eventing** 名 総合馬術《三日間をかけて馬場馬術, クロスカントリー, 障害飛び競技を行う種目》
- **every** 熟 once every four years

THE OLYMPIC FAQ

四年に一度

- **everyone** 代 誰でも, 皆
  everyone on Earth 誰でも, 全員
- **everything** 代 すべてのこと[もの], 何でも, 何もかも
- **everywhere** 副 どこにいても, いたるところに
- **example** 熟 for example たとえば
- **excavate** 動 発掘する
- **excavation** 名 発掘
- **excellent** 形 優れた, 優秀な
- **except** 前 〜以外は except for 〜 を除いて
- **excited** 形 興奮した, わくわくした get excited 興奮する
- **excitement** 名 興奮(すること)
- **exciting** 形 興奮させる, わくわくさせる
- **exercise** 名 ①運動, 体操 ②練習 動 運動する, 練習する
- **expect** 動 (当然のこととして)期待する, 予期[予測]する
- **expert** 名 専門家, 熟練者, エキスパート

F

- **facility** 名 《-ties》施設, 設備 public facility 公共施設
- **fact** 熟 in fact 実際のところ, 実は
- **fair** 形 正しい, 公平[正当]な fair play フェアプレー, 正々堂々と試合をすること
- **fairness** 名 公平さ, 公明正大さ
- **fall down** 転ぶ
- **fall in love with** 〜と恋におちる
- **fall off** (離れ)落ちる
- **fall to the ground** 転ぶ
- **famous for** 《be –》〜で有名である
- **fancy** 形 高価な, 高級な
- **FAQ** 略 よくある質問とその答え 《frequently asked questionsの略》
- **far from** 〜から遠い
- **far more** はるかに多く
- **faraway** 形 遠い, 遠方の
- **farmer** 名 農民, 農業従事者
- **farther** 副 もっと遠く, さらに先に
- **fat** 形 太った, 肥満の
- **feeling** 名 気持ち, 感情
- **fencing** 名 フェンシング
- **fiberglass** 名 ガラス繊維強化プラスチック
- **figure skating** フィギュアスケート
- **filled with** 《be –》〜でいっぱいになる
- **final** 形 最後の, 決定的な
- **finish line** (競争の)ゴール
- **Finland** 名 フィンランド《国名》
- **fitness** 名 (運動などによる)体の調子のよさ
- **five-sixths** 六分の五
- **flame** 名 炎 Olympic flame オリンピック聖火
- **flood** 名 洪水
- **floor exercise** (体操競技の)床運動
- **flute** 名 フルート《楽器》
- **football** 名 アメリカンフットボール
- **form** 名 形状, 状態 動 組織する
- **former** 形 《the –》(二者のうち)以前の
- **fortius** より強く《ラテン語, オリンピックのスローガンである, より速くより高くより強くの一つ》
- **France** 名 フランス《国名》

Word List

- **freedom** 名自由
- **freely** 副自由に, 勝手に
- **French** 形フランス(人)の 名フランス人
- **friendship** 名友情, 友達であること
- **frightening** 形恐ろしい, どきっとさせる
- **from ~ to ...** ～から…まで
- **Fujimoto, Shun** 藤本俊《体操競技選手, 日本。1976年膝を痛めながらも金メダルを獲得》
- **full of** 《be –》～で一杯である
- **funeral** 名葬式, 葬儀
- **funny** 形おもしろい, こっけいな
- **future** 熟 in the future 将来は

G

- **gather** 動集まる, 集める
- **Geneva** 名ジュネーヴ《スイス西部の都市》
- **George Eyser** ジョージ・エイゼル《体操選手, アメリカ。片足が義足であったにも関わらず, 1904年のオリンピックで一日に金メダル三つを含む六つものメダル獲得を果たした》
- **German** 形ドイツ(人)の 名ドイツ人
- **Germany** 名ドイツ《国名》
- **get back** 戻る, 帰る
- **get better** (病気などが)良くなる
- **get into** ～に入る
- **get sick** 病気になる
- **get to** ～に達する
- **giant** 形巨大な
- **gift** 名贈り物
- **give up** ～をあきらめる, 断念する, 放棄する
- **Giza** 名ギザ《エジプトの都市》

Great Pyramid of Giza ギザの大ピラミッド《ギザの三大ピラミッド中最古で最大のもの, 底辺230.4m, 高さ138.8m》

- **Glaucus** 名グラウコス《紀元前6世紀頃に名の知れていたボクサー》
- **glory** 名栄光, 名誉
- **go away** (病気が)治る
- **go back to** ～に帰る[戻る]
- **go up** 上がる
- **gold** 名金 形金の, 金製の
- **golf** 名ゴルフ
- **goods** 名財産, 所有物
- **gotten** 動get(得る)の過去分詞
- **graceful** 形優美な, 上品な
- **gram** 名グラム《重さの単位》
- **gray** 形青ざめた, 土色の
- **Great Britain** イギリス, 大ブリテン島《英国の主島》
- **Great Pyramid of Giza** ギザの大ピラミッド《ギザの三大ピラミッド中最古で最大のもの, 底辺230.4m, 高さ138.8m》
- **Greece** 名ギリシア《国名》
- **Greek** 形ギリシア(人・語)の 名ギリシア人
- **greet** 動あいさつする
- **Grenoble** 名グルノーブル《フランスの都市, 1968年冬季オリンピック開催地》
- **guideline** 名ガイドライン, 指針
- **gymnasium** 名体育館, 運動場, ギムナジウム
- **gymnast** 名体操選手
- **gymnastics** 名体操, 体操競技

H

- **halfway** 副中間[中途]で
- **Hans-Gunnar Liljenwall** ハ

The Olympic FAQ

ンス＝グンナー・リリエンヴァル《スウェーデン。1968年に近代五種種目で銅メダルを獲得するが、ドーピングが発覚し取り消された》
- □ **hard to** 〜し難い
- □ **harm** 動傷つける、損なう
- □ **head of** 〜の長 **head of state** 国家元首
- □ **headquarters** 名本部
- □ **healthy** 形健康な、健全な、健康によい
- □ **heatstroke** 名日射病、熱中症
- □ **Hellanodikai** 名ヘラノディカイ《古代オリンピックの審判官の名称》
- □ **hellene** 名（古代）ギリシア人
- □ **help 〜 to …** 〜が…するのを助ける
- □ **Helsinki** 名ヘルシンキ《フィンランドの首都、1952年夏季オリンピック開催地》
- □ **Henri Didon** アンリ・ディドン《オリンピック創設者であるクーベルタンの友人。元高校校長の修道士。1840–1900》
- □ **Hera** 名ヘラ《ギリシア神話の女神、ゼウスの妻》
- □ **Heracles** 名ヘラクレス《ギリシア神話の英雄、ゼウスの息子》
- □ **Heraea** 名古代の女性だけが参加できた運動競技大会
- □ **here is [are] 〜** こちらは〜です。
- □ **Herodotus** 名ヘロドトス《歴史の父と呼ばれている、古代ギリシアに生きた歴史家。紀元前五世紀ごろ》
- □ **highlight** 名見所、印象に残るできごと
- □ **Hippodamia** 名ヒッポダメイア《ギリシア神話に登場する女性、オイノマオス王の娘》
- □ **hippodrome** 名ヒッポドローム、古代の競技用走路
- □ **Hiroshima** 名広島《日本の都市、第二次世界大戦中に原子爆弾が投下された》
- □ **hobble** 動よろよろ歩く、片足を引きずって歩く
- □ **Homer** 名ホメロス《古代ギリシアの詩人、紀元前八世紀ごろ》
- □ **Hong Kong** 香港《中国の都市》
- □ **honor** 名名誉、栄誉 **in honor of** 〜に敬意を表して、〜を祝って、〜を記念して 動称える
- □ **hoplitodromia** 名武装競走《古代オリンピックの最終日に行われた、重い鎧を身に着けて競技場の周りを走るという競技》
- □ **host** 形主催の **host city** 開催都市 **host country** 開催国 動主催する
- □ **how to** 〜する方法
- □ **however** 接けれども、だが
- □ **Hubert Raudaschl** Hubert Raudaschl《セーリング選手、オーストリア。1964年から1996年にかけて九回連続でオリンピック出場を果たし、二度銀メダルを獲得》
- □ **hug** 動しっかりと抱き締める
- □ **huge** 形巨大な、ばく大な
- □ **hundreds of** 何百もの〜
- □ **Hungary** 名ハンガリー《国名》

I

- □ **Ian Millar** イアン・ミラー《馬術競技選手、カナダ。1972年から2008年まで九回のオリンピック出場を果たし、2008年に銀メダルを獲得》
- □ **ice hockey** アイスホッケー
- □ **if** 熟 **see if** 〜かどうかを確かめる
- □ **Igor Ter-Ovanesyan** イゴール・テルオバネシアン《陸上選手、旧ソビエト連邦。1960年と1964年に走り幅跳びで銅メダルを獲得》
- □ **imaging** 名イメージ、頭に思い浮かぶ画、映像
- □ **importance** 名重要性、大切さ

Word List

- **improve** 動改善する[させる], 進歩する
- **in fact** 実際のところ, 実は
- **in the end** 最後には, ついには
- **include** 動含む
- **incredible** 形信じられないほどすごい, すばらしい, とてつもない
- **individual** 形個人の
- **injure** 動傷つける, けがをさせる
- **injury** 名けが
- **Innsbruck** 名インスブルック《オーストリアの都市, 1976年冬季オリンピック開催地》
- **inspiration** 名鼓舞, 激励
- **instead of** ～の代わりに, ～をしないで
- **International Olympic committee** 国際オリンピック委員会《近代オリンピックを主催する非政府・非営利団体》
- **International Sports Week** 国際スポーツ週間《冬季オリンピックがまだなかった時代に, 国際オリンピック委員会が行っていた冬季種目の競技大会》
- **introduction** 名前書き, 序論
- **IOC** 略国際オリンピック委員会《近代オリンピックを主催する非政府・非営利団体。International Olympic committeeの略》
- **Iphitos** 名イピトス《古代オリンピックを提唱したと伝説に伝えられている王》
- **Israel** 名イスラエル《国名》
- **Israeli** 形イスラエル(人)の 名イスラエル人
- **Isthmian Games** イストミア大祭《古代ギリシアで行われていた競技大会の一つ。二年に一度開催されていた》
- **It is ～ for someone to …** (人)が…するのは～だ
- **It takes someone ～ to …** (人)が…するのに～(時間など)がかかる
- **Italy** 名イタリア《国名》
- **ivory** 名象牙

J

- **jail** 名刑務所
- **Jamaica** 名ジャマイカ《国名》
- **javelin** 名 (投げ槍用の) 槍
- **Jeannie Longo** ジャニー・ロンゴ《自転車競技選手, フランス。七度オリンピックに出場, 1996年に金メダルを獲得し, 続く三つのオリンピックでも銀メダルを獲得》
- **jewel** 名宝石
- **Jim Abbot** ジム・アボット《野球選手, アメリカ。先天的に右手がなかったが, 投手として活躍し1988年チームを金メダルに導いた》
- **Jim Peters** ジム・ピーターズ《陸上選手, イギリス。長距離走やマラソンで新記録を更新した著名な選手》
- **Jim Thorpe** ジム・ソープ《スポーツ選手, アメリカ。1912年に陸上競技で二つの金メダルを獲るが, 過去にプロ球界に出場していたことからアマチュア資格を失効し取り消された》
- **Johann Rosenzopf** Johann Rosenzopf《ユースオリンピックのアイデアを最初に考えた人。1939–》
- **journalist** 名報道関係者, ジャーナリスト
- **judge** 動審判する, 名審判
- **judo** 名柔道
- **jump up and down** 飛び跳ねる
- **jumper** 名跳ぶ人, 跳躍選手
- **just as** (ちょうど)であろうとおり

THE OLYMPIC FAQ

K

- **keep someone from** ～から（人）を阻む
- **kidnap** 動 誘拐する
- **kilogram** 名 キログラム《重量の単位》
- **kilometer** 名 キロメートル《長さの単位》
- **kind** 熟 all kinds of さまざまな，あらゆる種類の
- **kiss** 動 キスする
- **knee** 名 ひざ
- **know if** ～かどうかを知る
- **Knud Enemark Jensen** クヌート・エネマルク・イェンセン《自転車競技選手，デンマーク。1960年のオリンピックで興奮剤の一種を摂取して競技に出場し，急死した》
- **kotinos** 名 古代オリンピックで優勝者に授与された，オリーブの枝で作られた冠

L

- **Lake Placid** レークプラシッド《アメリカの都市，1932年と1980年の冬季オリンピック開催地》
- **landowner** 名 地主
- **Latin** 名 ラテン語
- **Lausanne** 名 ローザンヌ《スイスの都市，国際オリンピック委員会の本拠地》
- **lawn tennis** ローンテニス《芝生のコートで行うテニス》
- **Lawrence Lremieux** ローレンス・レミュー《ヨット競技選手，カナダ。1988年のオリンピック中，競技中に海に落ちた他の選手を救助し，特別賞を授与された》
- **lay** 動 lie（横たわる）の過去 **lie down** 横たわる，横になる
- **lazy** 形 怠惰な，怠慢な
- **least** 熟 at least 少なくとも
- **legend** 名 伝説，伝説的人物，言い伝え
- **length** 名 長さ，距離
- **less** 形 より小さい［少ない］
- **let go of** ～から手を離す
- **level** 名 水準，レベル
- **Lewis, Carl** （カール・）ルイス《陸上選手，アメリカ。1984年～1996年の間に短距離走，リレー，走り幅飛びなどで九つの金メダルと一つの銀メダルを獲得した》
- **life** 熟 for the rest of life 死ぬまで
- **lift** 動 持ち上げる
- **like this** このような，こんなふうに
- **likely** 形 ありそうな 副 たぶん，おそらく **very likely** たぶん
- **Lillehammer** 名 リレハンメル《ノルウェーの都市，1994年冬季オリンピック開催地》
- **Lina Radke** リナ・ラトケ《陸上選手，ドイツ。女子陸上の草分け的存在。1928年に金メダルを獲得》
- **list** 名 目録，一覧表
- **lit** 動 light（火をつける）の過去，過去分詞
- **little by little** 少しずつ
- **lives** 熟 once in their lives 一生に一度は
- **loincloth** 名 腰巻，ふんどし
- **London** 名 ロンドン《英国の首都》
- **long-distance race** 長距離走
- **Los Angeles** ロサンゼルス《米国の都市》
- **love** 熟 fall in love with ～恋におちる
- **Ludwig Guttmann** ルートヴィヒ・グットマン《医師，パラリンピックの提唱者。1899–1980》
- **Lynn Davies** リン・デイビーズ《走り幅跳び選手，英国。1964年金メ

Word List

ダルを獲得》

M

- **main** 形 主な, 主要な
- **make** 熟 be made of ～でできて[作られて]いる be made out of ～でできている be made up of ～で構成されている make into ～を…に仕立てる make out 作り上げる make sure 確かめる, 確認する
- **marathon** 名 マラソン
- **marble** 名 大理石
- **march** 動 行軍する, 進攻する
- **Marla Runyan** マーラ・ランヤン《陸上選手, アメリカ。視覚障害でほとんど目が見えなかったが, 2000年に1500メートル走に出場した》
- **married** 形 結婚した, 既婚の
- **marry** 動 結婚する
- **massage** 名 マッサージ
- **match** 名 試合, 勝負
- **material** 名 材料, 原料
- **mathematics** 名 数学
- **matter** 熟 not matter 問題にならない
- **meaning** 名 意味, 趣旨
- **measure** 動 計る
- **medal** 名 メダル
- **medical** 形 医療の, 医学の
- **meeting** 名 集まり, 会議, ミーティング
- **Melbourne** 名 メルボルン《オーストラリアの都市, 1956年夏季オリンピック開催地》
- **mental** 形 心の, 精神的な
- **Merlene Ottey** マリーン・オッティ《陸上選手, ジャマイカ→スロベニア。1980年から2004年までオリンピックに出場し, 計九つもの銅, 銀メダルを獲得した》
- **messenger** 名 使者, 伝達者
- **metal** 名 金属, 合金
- **meter** 名 メートル《長さの単位》
- **method** 名 方法, 手段
- **Mexico** 名 メキシコ《国名》
- **Michael Phelps** マイケル・フェルプス《水泳選手, アメリカ。2004年に六つ, 2008年に八つの金メダルを獲得した》
- **might** 助《mayの過去》～かもしれない
- **millimeter** 名 ミリメートル《長さの単位》
- **Milo of Croton** クロトンのミロ《古代オリンピックのレスリング選手, 20年間の五大会で優勝し続けたといわれている》
- **mind** 名 心, 精神
- **mirror** 名 鏡
- **modern** 形 現代[近代]の, 現代的な, 最近の
- **moment** 名 瞬間, (ごく短い)時間
- **Montreal** 名 モントリオール《カナダの都市, 1976年夏季オリンピック開催地》
- **more** 熟 far more はるかに多く more and more ますます more than ～以上 not ～ any more もう[これ以上]～ない
- **Moscow** 名 モスクワ《ロシアの首都》
- **most** 熟 at (the) most せいぜい, 多くても
- **mostly** 副 主として, ほとんど
- **motion** 名 動き, 運動 spirit in motion 躍動する魂
- **motto** 名 座右の銘, 標語, モットー
- **moved** 熟《be-》感激する, 感銘する
- **Much Wenlock** マッチ・ウェンロック《イギリス中部に位置する町, この町で行われていた競技大会が近

代オリンピックのヒントになったといわれている》
- **Muhammad Ali** モハメド・アリ《ボクサー、アメリカ。1960年ローマオリンピック・ライトヘビー級金メダリスト。WBAヘビー級王座を三度獲得した史上初の人》
- **Munich** 图ミュンヘン《ドイツの都市、1972年夏季オリンピック開催地》
- **muscle** 图筋肉、腕力
- **museum** 图博物館、美術館
- **myth** 图神話

N

- **Nadia Comaneci** ナディア・コマネチ《体操選手、ルーマニア。1976年に体操競技で史上初の10点満点を記録し、三つの金メダルを獲得。1980年にも二つの金メダルを獲得》
- **Nagano** 图長野《1998年冬季オリンピック開催地》
- **narrow** 形狭く限られた
- **Natalie du Toit** ナタリー・デュトワ《競泳選手、南アフリカ。片足を失っているが、2008年に肢を失っている人として初めてのオリンピック出場を果たした》
- **nation** 图国
- **national** 形国家[国民]の
- **natural science** 自然科学
- **nearly** 副ほとんど
- **necessary** 形必要な、不可欠な
- **need to do** ～する必要がある
- **Nemea** 图ネメア《古代ギリシアの都市》
- **Nemean Games** ネメアー大祭《古代の競技大会の一つで二年に一度開催されていた》
- **nervous** 形神経過敏な、不安定な
- **Netherlands** 图オランダ《国名》
- **news** 图ニュース、注目すべき事件
- **normal** 形普通の、通常の 图平常、標準
- **Norway** 图ノルウェー《国名》
- **number** 熟 great numbers of ものすごい数の～

O

- **oath** 图宣誓、誓い
- **obvious** 形明らかな、明白な
- **Oceania** 图オーストラリア大陸とニュージーランドその周辺の島々、太平洋の島々をあわせた地域
- **Oenomaus** 图オイノマオス《ギリシア神話に登場する王の名前》
- **official rules** 公認規則
- **officially** 副公式に、正式に
- **oil** 图油
- **olive** 图オリーブ
- **Olympia** 图オリンピア《古代ギリシアの都市、古代オリンピックが行われた場所》
- **Olympiad** 图オリンピア紀、オリンピックを数えるための四年ごとの暦
- **Olympian** 图オリンピック選手
- **Olympic** 图オリンピック《四年に一度開催される世界的な運動競技大会。冬季と夏季がある》
- **Olympic Charter** 五輪憲章
- **Olympic flame** オリンピック聖火
- **Olympic truce** オリンピック停戦
- **once every four years** 四年に一度
- **once in their lives** 一生に一度は
- **one another** お互い
- **one-hundredth** 百分の一

WORD LIST

- **oneself** 熟 自分自身 by oneself 一人で, 自分だけで for oneself 独力で, 自分のために
- **only** 熟 not only ~ but (also) … ~だけでなく…もまた
- **onto** 前 ~の上へ[に]
- **opening** 形 開会の opening ceremony 開会式
- **ordinary** 形 一般の, 平凡な
- **organization** 名 組織, 団体, 機関
- **organize** 動 組織する
- **origin** 名 起源
- **original** 形 始めの, 元の
- **originally** 副 もともとは, はじめは
- **Orsippos of Megara** メガラのオルシッポス《古代オリンピックの陸上選手》
- **Oscar Swahn** オスカー・スワン《射撃選手, スウェーデン。1912年に最長齢の金メダリストになった》
- **Oslo** 名 オスロ《ノルウェーの首都, 1952年冬季オリンピック開催地》
- **other** 熟 all the others 他の全員を
- **out** 熟 make out 作り上げる 9.5 out of 10 10人の9.5点
- **outdoor** 形 戸外の
- **outdoors** 副 戸外で
- **over** 熟 be over 終わる over time 時間とともに, そのうち
- **owner** 名 持ち主, オーナー
- **oxen** 名 ox (雄牛) の複数形

P

- **pace** 名 速度, ペース
- **paidotribai** 名 古代オリンピック選手たちの専属のコーチ
- **painful** 形 痛い, 痛ましい
- **painting** 名 絵(をかくこと), 絵画
- **Palestinian** 名 パレスチナ人
- **pan** allを意味するギリシア語
- **Panhellenic Games** パンヘレニック競技会《古代ギリシアで行われていた四つの競技会の総称》
- **pankration** 名 パンクラチオン《古代オリンピックで行われていた格闘技のような種目》
- **para** besideを意味するギリシア語
- **parade** 名 パレード, 行進
- **Paralympic** 名 パラリンピック《四年に一度開催される身体障害者のための国際的スポーツ競技大会》
- **Paris** 名 パリ《フランスの首都, 1900年と1924年の夏季オリンピック開催地》
- **Parkinson's Disease** パーキンソン病《体が震えたり, 動作が思うようにできなくなる難病》
- **part** 熟 take part in ~に参加する
- **participate** 動 参加する, 加わる
- **pass down** (次の世代に)伝える
- **past** 形 過去の, この前の 名 過去
- **pay** 動 (給料を)支払う, 報いる
- **peaceful** 形 平和な, 穏やかな
- **peak** 名 頂点, 最高点
- **PEDs** 略 運動能力向上薬《performance-enhancing drugsの略》
- **Pelops** 名 ペロプス《ギリシア神話に登場する英雄で, オリンピックの祖とされる伝説が残っている》
- **pentathlon** 名 ペンタスロン, 五種競技《五種目の競技からなる種目で, 古代近代どちらのオリンピックにもあるが, 競技の内容は少し異なる》
- **perfectly** 副 完璧に, 申し分なく
- **perform** 動 ①(競技などを)行う ②上演する
- **performance** 名 演技, 演目 ②成績

The Olympic FAQ

- **performance-enhancing drugs** 運動能力向上薬
- **perhaps** 副 たぶん, もしかすると
- **period** 名 期間, 時間
- **physiotherapy** 名 理学療法
- **pick up** 持ち上げる
- **Pierre de Coubertin** ピエール・ド・クーベルタン《近代オリンピックの提唱, 創設者。1863–1937》
- **pitcher** 名 投手, ピッチャー
- **place** 熟 take place 行われる, 起こる
- **plan to do** ～するつもりである
- **planning** 名 計画, 設計
- **plaque** 名 飾り板
- **plate** 名 金属板, プレート
- **player** 名 競技者, 選手
- **plow** 名 鋤, プラウ《農具》Give him one for the plow! 鋤にくれてやった一発をあいつにも食らわせてやれ！
- **poet** 名 詩人
- **poetry** 名 詩歌, 詩を書くこと
- **pole** 名 棒, さお, ポール
- **policy** 名 方針
- **Polites** 名 ポリーテース《古代オリンピックの陸上選手, 長距離走と短距離走の両方で優勝したといわれている》
- **political** 形 政治の, 政治的な
- **politics** 名 政治, 政略
- **pommel horse** (体操競技の)鞍馬
- **pool** 名 プール
- **Poseidon** 名 ポセイドン《ギリシア神話の海をつかさどる神》
- **possible** 形 ①可能な ②ありうる, 起こりうる
- **pottery** 名 陶器
- **powder** 名 おしろい, 粉
- **powerful** 形 実力のある, 影響力のある
- **preparation** 名 準備, したく
- **prepare for** ～の準備をする
- **presentation** 名 プレゼンテーション, 発表
- **president** 名 会長
- **pressure** 名 プレッシャー, 圧力, 重荷
- **prevent** 動 予防する, 防ぐ
- **price** 名 《-s》物価, 相場
- **priestess** 名 巫女, 女性の祭司
- **prisoner** 名 収監者, 投獄された人
- **probably** 副 たぶん, あるいは
- **professional** 形 プロの, 職業的な 名 プロ選手
- **Prometheus** 名 プロメテウス《ギリシア神話の神, ゼウスの火を盗み人間に与えたとされる》
- **promote** 動 ①促進する ②売り込む
- **protest** 動 抗議する
- **province** 名 属州
- **public** 形 公共の public facility 公共施設 public transportation system 公共交通機関
- **punch** 名 パンチ, 一撃
- **pure** 形 純粋な, けがれのない
- **purity** 名 汚れのないこと, 清浄, 純粋
- **purple** 形 紫色の
- **put in** ～の中に入れる
- **put on** ～を体につける
- **Pyeongchang** 名 平昌(ピョンチャン)《韓国の都市, 2018年冬季オリンピック開催予定地》
- **pyramid** 名 ピラミッド Great Pyramid of Giza ギザの大ピラミッド《ギザの三大ピラミッド中最古で最大のもの。底辺230.4m, 高さ138.8m》
- **Pythian Games** ピューティア

Word List

大祭《古代ギリシアで行われていた四つの競技大会のうちの一つ。四年に一度開催されていた》

Q

- **qualify** 動資格を得る[与える]
- **qualifying race** 予選レース
- **quickly** 副急速に, 速く, すぐに
- **quit** 動やめる, 辞職する, 中止する

R

- **racist** 形人種差別主義の, 民族主義の
- **raise** 動上げる, 掲げる
- **ray** 名光線
- **realize** 動気づく, 悟る
- **reason for** ～の理由
- **rebirth** 名復興, 再生
- **recent** 形近ごろの, 近代の
- **recently** 副近ごろ, 最近
- **recommend** 動勧める
- **record** 名記録
- **record-breaking** 形新記録の
- **rediscover** 動再発見する, 見直す
- **refuse** 動拒絶する, 断る
- **regular** 形正規の, 通常の
- **related** 形関係のある, 関連した
- **relationship** 名関係, 結びつき
- **relay** 名リレー　torch relay 聖火リレー
- **release** 動解放する, 釈放する
- **religion** 名宗教
- **religious** 形宗教の, 宗教的な
- **remove** 動取り去る, 取りやめる
- **replace** 動取り替える
- **reporter** 名記者, リポーター
- **represent** 動象徴する, 表す
- **rescue** 動救助する, 助ける
- **reservation** 名予約, 指定　seat reservation 座席指定
- **respect** 名尊敬, 尊重 動尊敬[尊重]する
- **rest** 熟 for the rest of life 死ぬまで
- **retired** 形退職した, 引退した
- **Rhea** 名レア《ギリシア神話の女神, ゼウスの母》
- **rhythm** 名リズム, 調子
- **Richard Chandler** リチャード・チャンドラー《オリンピアの遺跡を発見した考古学者。1738–1810》
- **riding** 名乗馬
- **ring** 名輪, 円形 ②体操競技のつり輪
- **Rio de Janeiro** リオデジャネイロ《ブラジルの都市, 2016年夏季オリンピック開催予定地》
- **rival** 名競争相手
- **robe** 名《-s》式服, 法衣
- **Robert Legendre** ロバート・ルジャンドル《スポーツ選手, アメリカ。1924年五種競技で銅メダルを獲得, その中の走り幅跳びでは世界記録を更新した》
- **Roman** 形ローマ(人)の 名ローマ人[市民]
- **Roman Empire** 古代ローマ帝国の皇帝
- **Romania** 名ルーマニア《国名》
- **Rome** 名①ローマ《イタリアの首都》②古代ローマ(帝国)
- **routine** 名型にはまった一連の演技
- **rower** 名ボート選手
- **rowing** 名ボート競技
- **Rugby** 名ラグビー校《イギリスにある歴史ある学校, ラグビー発祥の地といわれている》

- **ruin** 名 廃墟, 旧跡
- **run around** 走り回る
- **run down** 駆け下りる
- **run out** 走り出る
- **runner** 名 走者, ランナー
- **running** 名 ランニング, 競走
  running track 陸上競技用トラック
- **Russia** 名 ロシア《国名》
- **Russian** 名 ロシア人

S

- **sacred** 形 神聖な
- **sacrifice** 名 神に生け贄をささげること
- **sadly** 副 悲しいことに, 残念ながら
- **safely** 副 安全に
- **safety** 名 安全
- **sailing** 名 帆走, セーリング, ヨット競技
- **sailor** 名 船員, ヨット競技選手
- **Sapporo** 名 札幌《1972年冬季オリンピック開催地》
- **Sarajevo** 名 サラエヴォ《旧ユーゴスラビアの都市で現ボスニアヘルツェゴビナの首都, ユーゴ時代の1984年に冬季オリンピックが開催された》
- **scandal** 名 スキャンダル, 不祥事, 醜聞
- **scary** 形 恐ろしい, こわい
- **schedule** 名 予定, スケジュール 動 予定を立てる
- **score** 名 (競技の)得点, スコア 動 (競技で)得点する, 採点する
- **scoreboard** 名 得点表示板, スコアボード
- **sculpture** 名 彫刻, 彫刻作品
- **seat reservation** 座席予約
- **second-largest** 二番目に大きい
- **security** 名 安全(性)

- **see if** ～かどうかを確かめる
- **seem** 動 (～に)見える **seem to be** ～であるように思われる
- **Seiko Hashimoto** 橋本聖子《日本。スピードスケートと自転車競技で夏季, 冬季両方のオリンピックに計七回出場し, 1992年スピードスケートで銅メダルを獲得》
- **select** 動 選択する, 選ぶ
- **self-respect** 名 自尊(心)
- **send out** 使いに出す, 派遣する
- **sensor** 名 感知装置, センサー
- **Seoul** 名 ソウル《韓国の首都, 1988年夏季オリンピック開催地》
- **serious** 形 ①まじめな, 真剣な ②重大な, 深刻な
- **Seven Wonders of the Ancient World** 古代世界の七不思議
- **shake** 動 揺れる, 震える
- **shameful** 形 恥ずべき, 面目丸潰れな
- **shark** 名 サメ(鮫)
- **shelter** 名 避難所, 避難小屋
- **shocking** 形 衝撃的な, ショッキングな
- **shoelace** 名 靴ひも
- **shooting** 名 射撃
- **short-distance** 短距離の
- **show ～ how to ...** ～に…のやり方を示す
- **Shun Fujimoto** 藤本俊《体操競技選手, 日本。1976年膝を痛めながらも金メダルを獲得》
- **shy** 形 内気な, 恥ずかしがりの
- **sick** 熟 **get sick** 病気になる
- **sickness** 名 病気
- **side** 名 横, そば
- **silent** 形 ①無言の, 黙っている ②静かな, 音を立てない
- **silver** 名 銀 形 銀製の

Word List

- **similar to** 《be –》〜に似ている
- **Singapore** 名 シンガポール《国名》
- **Singaporean** 名 シンガポール人
- **single** 形 たった1つの
- **situation** 名 状況, 境遇
- **skater** 名 スケート選手
- **skating** 名 スケート(をすること)
- **ski** 名 スキー 動 スキーをする
- **skiing** 名 スキー(をすること)
- **skill** 名 技能, 技術
- **slippery** 形 つるつる滑る, 滑りやすい
- **Slovenia** 名 スロヴェニア《国名》
- **slow down** 速度を落とす
- **slowly** 副 遅く, ゆっくり
- **smoke** 名 煙
- **sneak** 動 こそこそする sneak away こっそり立ち去る sneak in こっそり入る
- **snuck** 動 sneak(こそこそする)の過去形
- **so that** 〜できるように
- **Sochi** 名 ソチ《ロシアの都市, 2014年冬季オリンピック開催予定地》
- **society** 名 社会
- **soldier** 名 兵士, 軍人
- **someday** 副 いつか, そのうち
- **somehow** 副 ①どうにかこうにか, ともかく, 何とかして ②どういうわけか
- **someone** 代 ある人, 誰か
- **somersault** 名 宙返り, とんぼ返り
- **something** 代 ①ある物, 何か ②いくぶん, 多少
- **sometime** 副 いつか, そのうち
- **sometimes** 副 時々, ときには
- **South Korea** 韓国
- **Soviet Union** ソビエト社会主義共和国連邦《通称ソ連, 1991年に解体》
- **Spain** 名 スペイン《国名》
- **spar** 動 スパーリング(実践に近い形式の練習)をする
- **specially** 副 特別に
- **spectator** 名 観客, 見物人
- **speech** 熟 make a speech 演説をする
- **speech-making** 演説
- **speed** 名 速力, 速度
- **speed skating** スピードスケート《スケートリンクを周回し, ゴールまでのタイムを競う》
- **spirit** 名 精神, 魂
- **spirit in motion** 躍動する魂《パラリンピックのモットー》
- **sponsor** 名 スポンサー, 出資者, 広告主 動 スポンサーになる, 出資する
- **Sports Illustrated** スポーツ・イラストレイテッド《アメリカで人気のあるスポーツ週刊誌》
- **sportsman** 名 スポーツマン, 運動家
- **sportsmanship** 名 スポーツマンシップ, 正々堂々と勝負する精神
- **spot** 名 地点, 場所 on the spot その場で
- **sprint** 名 短距離競争, スプリント
- **sprinter** 名 短距離走者
- **Squaw valley** スコーバレー《アメリカの都市, 1960年冬季オリンピック開催地》
- **St. Louis** セントルイス《アメリカの都市, 1904年夏季オリンピック開催地》
- **St. Moritz** サンモリッツ《スイスの都市, 1928年と1948年に冬季オリンピックが開催された》
- **stade** 名 スタディオン走《古代オリンピックで行われていた短距離走の

一種》
- **stadium** 名 スタジアム, 競技場
- **state** 名 ①国家 head of state 国家元首 ②(自治)州
- **statue** 名 像
- **stay away from** ～から離れている
- **stay in** (場所)に泊まる, 滞在する
- **step** 熟 take short steps 小刻みに歩く
- **steroid** 名 ステロイド, 筋肉増強剤の一種
- **stimulate** 動 活性化させる
- **Stockholm** 名 ストックホルム《スウェーデンの首都, 1912年夏季オリンピック開催地》
- **stole** 動 steal (盗む) の過去
- **straighten** 動 まっすぐにする
- **strength** 名 力, 体力
- **stress** 名 精神的重圧, ストレス
- **stretcher** 名 担架
- **strict** 形 厳しい, 厳密な
- **strychnine** 名 ストリキニーネ《興奮作用を持つ非常に毒性の強い薬物》
- **subway** 名 地下鉄
- **success** 名 成功
- **successful** 形 成功した, うまくいった
- **such ~ that ...** 非常に～なので…
- **such as** たとえば～, ～のような
- **suffer** 動 苦しむ, 悩む
- **suit** 名 ①スーツ ②ひとそろい, 一組 suits of armor よろい一式
- **superhuman** 形 超人的な, 神わざの
- **supervise** 動 監督する
- **support** 動 支える, 援助する 名 援助, 支え
- **suppose** 動 《be -d to ～》～することになっている, ～するものである
- **sure** 熟 make sure 確かめる, 確認する
- **surprising** 形 驚くべき
- **surprisingly** 副 驚くべきことに, 意外にも
- **survey** 名 調査
- **survive** 動 生き残る, 生き延びる
- **swam** 動 swim (泳ぐ) の過去形
- **sweat** 名 汗 動 汗をかく
- **Sweden** 名 スウェーデン《国名》
- **Swedish** 形 スウェーデン人の
- **swimmer** 名 水泳選手
- **swimming** 名 水泳
- **Swiss** 名 スイス人
- **Switzerland** 名 スイス《国名》
- **Sydney** 名 シドニー《オーストラリアの都市, 2000年夏季オリンピック開催地》
- **symbol** 名 シンボル, 象徴
- **symbolize** 動 象徴する, 象徴とみなす

T

- **Tae kwon do** テコンドー《多彩な蹴り技が特徴的な韓国の格闘技》
- **take part in** ～に参加する
- **take place** 行われる
- **take short steps** 小刻みに歩く
- **talented** 形 才能のある, 有能な
- **Tara Lipinski** タラ・リピンスキー《フィギュアスケート選手, アメリカ。1998年に史上最年少の金メダリストとなった》
- **tax** 名 税
- **technique** 名 テクニック, 技術, 手法
- **technology** 名 テクノロジー, 科学技術

Word List

- **temple** 名神殿, 寺院
- **tennis** 名テニス
- **tent** 名テント, 天幕
- **tenth of** 《a-》~の10分の1
- **terminal** 名起点・終点駅, ターミナル
- **terrorism** 名テロ行為, 武力行為
- **terrorist** 名テロリスト
- **testing** 名テストすること, 検査
- **than any other** ほかのどの~よりも
- **thanks to** ~のおかげで
- **Theodosius** 名テオドシウス帝《古代ローマ帝国の皇帝》
- **these days** このごろ
- **think of** ~を思いつく, 考え出す
- **thinking** 名考え, 思考
- **Thomas Hicks** トーマス・ヒックス《陸上選手, アメリカ。1904年にマラソンで金メダルを獲得したが, 実は競技中に薬物を摂取していた(当時のルールには抵触しなかった)》
- **those day** 《in-》その当時は
- **though** 副しかし **even though** ~であるけれども, ~にもかかわらず
- **thousands of** 何千という
- **throne** 名王座
- **through** 前①~じゅうを, ~の全体を通して ②~を通じて, ~を用いて ③~を通り抜けて
- **throughout** 前~中, ~を通じて 副初めから終わりまで, ずっと
- **Thucydides** 名トゥキディデス《紀元前五世紀ごろの古代アテネの歴史家》
- **time** 熟 **all the time** ずっと, いつも, その間ずっと **at the time** そのころ, 当時は **in time with** ~に合わせて **over time** 時間とともに, そのうち
- **tiny** 形とても小さい
- **tired** 形疲労した, 消耗した
- **Tokyo** 名東京《1964年夏季オリンピック開催地》
- **torch** 名たいまつ **torch relay** 聖火リレー
- **Torino** 名トリノ《イタリアの都市, 2006年冬季オリンピック開催地》
- **total** 形完全な 名全体, 合計
- **totally** 副全体的に, すっかり
- **tough** 形①骨の折れる, 大変な ②頑丈な, 不屈な, タフな
- **tourism** 名観光業
- **tourist** 名旅行者, 観光客 **tourist attraction** 観光名所
- **track** 名競走路, トラック **running track** 陸上競技用トラック
- **track and field** 陸上競技
- **trainer** 名トレーナー, 指導者
- **training** 名トレーニング, 訓練
- **transportation** 名交通(機関) **public transportation system** 公共交通機関
- **treasure** 名貴重品, 宝物
- **tricky** 形巧妙な
- **truce** 名一時休戦, 停戦協定
- **truly** 副本当に, 真に
- **tug of war** 綱引き

U

- **understanding** 名理解, 意見の一致, 了解
- **uneven bar** 段違い平行棒(体操競技の一種目)
- **unfair** 形不公平な
- **unfortunately** 副不幸にも, 運悪く
- **union** 名①連合, 団体 ②連合国家
- **Union of French Athletic Clubs** 後に近代オリンピックを提

The Olympic FAQ

唱するクーベルタンが1887年に組織したフランスのスポーツクラブ連盟

- **United States** 名アメリカ合衆国《国名》
- **unless** 接もし~でなければ、~しなければ
- **untie** 動ほどく
- **untrue** 形真実でない、事実に反する
- **unusual** 形普通でない、珍しい、見[聞き]慣れない
- **Usain Bolt** ウサイン・ボルト《陸上選手、ジャマイカ。2008年に短距離走で三つの金メダルを獲得、100メートル走と200メートル走では世界新記録を出した》
- **USSR** 略ソビエト社会主義共和国連邦、Union of Soviet Socialist Republicsの略

V

- **value** 名価値、値打ち
- **Vancouver** 名バンクーバー《カナダの都市、2010年冬季オリンピック開催地》
- **various** 形変化に富んだ、さまざまの、たくさんの
- **vault** 名跳躍、飛び越え
- **version** 名バージョン、版
- **victory** 名勝利、優勝
- **viewer** 名視聴者、観戦者
- **visitor** 名訪問客、観光客
- **volleyball** 名バレーボール

W

- **WADA** 略世界反ドーピング機構《World Anti-Doping Agencyの略、スポーツにおける薬物使用への反対運動を推進する機構》
- **walk around** 歩き回る、ぶらぶら歩く
- **war** 熟 at war 戦争中、交戦中
- **warm-up** 準備運動
- **watch over** 見守る、見張る
- **way** 熟 all the way ずっと、はるばる、いろいろと in this way このようにして way to ~する方法
- **weapon** 名武器、兵器
- **wedding** 名結婚式、婚礼
- **weigh** 動重さが~ある
- **weight** 名おもり、おもし
- **weightlifter** 名重量挙げ選手
- **weightlifting** 名重量挙げ
- **well** 熟 as well なお、その上、同様に do well 成績が良い、成功する
- **wheelchair** 名車いす
- **wherever** 接どこでも、どこへ~するとも
- **whether** 接~かどうか
- **while** 熟 after a while しばらくして
- **whip** 動むちうつ 名むち
- **whole** 形全体の、すべての 名《the -》全体、全部
- **wide** 形幅が~ある
- **William Penny Brookes** ウィリアム・ペニー・ブルックス《医師、近代オリンピックの提唱者であるクーベルタンに、その元となるアイデアを与えた。1809-1895》
- **willpower** 名意思の力、自制心
- **Wimbledon** ウィンブルドン《イギリスの都市、テニスの四大国際大会の開催地の一つ》
- **win against** ~に勝つ、~を打ち負かす
- **winner** 名勝者
- **winning** 名勝利、勝つこと、勝ち取ること 形勝った、優勝の
- **wonder** 動不思議に思う、(~

Word List

- に)驚く 图不思議なもの **seven wonders** 七不思議
- **wooden** 形木製の, 木でできた
- **workout** 图練習, トレーニング
- **World Anti-Doping Agency** 世界反ドーピング機構《スポーツにおける薬物使用への反対運動を推進する機構》
- **worry about** 〜のことを心配する
- **worse** 副いっそう悪く
- **worship** 動崇拝する, 礼拝[参拝]する
- **worst** 形《the -》いちばんひどい
- **worth** 形(〜の)価値がある 图価値, 値打ち
- **wreath** 图花輪, リース
- **wrestling** 图レスリング
- **writer** 图作家

Y

- **yacht** 图ヨット
- **year** 熟 for years 何年も
- **Yoshinori Sakai** 坂井義則《陸上選手, 日本。オリンピック出場選手ではなかったが, 1964年東京オリンピックの聖火リレーでアンカーを務めた》
- **youth** 图若者
- **Youth Olympic Games** ユース五輪《14歳から18歳までを対象とした青少年向けのオリンピック》
- **Yugoslavia** 图ユーゴスラビア《東ヨーロッパに存在していた国家, 1929–2003》

Z

- **Zappas Olympics** ザッパスオリンピック《19世紀後半にギリシアで行われていた運動競技大会》
- **Zeus** 图ゼウス《ギリシア神話に登場する神々の王》

E-CAT

English **C**onversational **A**bility **T**est
国際英語会話能力検定

● E-CATとは…
英語が話せるようになるための
テストです。インターネット
ベースで、30分であなたの発
話力をチェックします。

www.ecatexam.com

iTEP

● iTEP®とは…
世界各国の企業、政府機関、アメリカの大学
300校以上が、英語能力判定テストとして採用。
オンラインによる90分のテストで文法、リー
ディング、リスニング、ライティング、スピー
キングの5技能をスコア化。iTEP®は、留学、就
職、海外赴任などに必要な、世界に通用する英
語を総合的に評価する画期的なテストです。

www.itepexamjapan.com

ラダーシリーズ
The Olympic FAQ　オリンピック FAQ

2012 年 7 月 2 日　第 1 刷発行
2020 年 3 月 10 日　第 2 刷発行

著　者　ジェイク・ロナルドソン

発行者　浦　晋亮

発行所　IBC パブリッシング株式会社
　　　　〒162-0804 東京都新宿区中里町 29 番 3 号
　　　　菱秀神楽坂ビル 9 F
　　　　Tel. 03-3513-4511　Fax. 03-3513-4512
　　　　www.ibcpub.co.jp

© IBC Publishing. Inc. 2012

印刷　株式会社シナノパブリッシングプレス
装丁　伊藤 理恵
カバー写真　portokalis / 123RF ストックフォト　　本文写真　wikipedia, 他
組版データ　Sabon Roman + Myriad Pro Semibold

落丁本・乱丁本は、小社宛にお送りください。送料小社負担にてお取り替えいたします。本書の無断複写(コピー)は著作権法上での例外を除き禁じられています。

Printed in Japan
ISBN978-4-7946-0150-6